Thomas Jefferson

Thomas Jefferson

Jacqueline Ching

DK PUBLISHING

LONDON, NEW YORK, MUNICH,
MELBOURNE, AND DELHI

Editor : Beth Landis Hester
Publishing Director : Beth Sutinis
Designer : Mark Johnson Davies
Managing Art Editor : Michelle Baxter
Production Controller : Jen Lockwood
DTP Coordinator : Kathy Farias
Photo Research : Anne Burns Images

First American Edition, 2009

09 10 11 12 13 10 9 8 7 6 5 4 3 2
Published in the United States
by DK Publishing
375 Hudson Street
New York, New York 10014

DK books are available at special discounts
when purchased in bulk for sales
promotions, premiums, fund-raising,
or educational use. For details, contact:

DK Publishing Special Markets
375 Hudson Street
New York, New York 10014
SpecialSales@dk.com

A catalog record for this book is available
from the Library of Congress.

ISBN 978-0-7566-4506-9 (Paperback)
ISBN 978-0-7566-4505-2 (Hardcover)

Printed and bound in China
by South China Printing Co., Ltd.

Discover more at
www.dk.com

Contents

Calm and Turbulence

Thomas Jefferson knelt down, looking through his telescope for signs of invasion. He had been warned: The British were on their way to Charlottesville. The next stop after that would be his home, Monticello. Would the British burn his house? Was there time to save his precious documents? It was June 1781, and British Lieutenant Colonel Banastre Tarleton, nicknamed "Bloody Ban" or "Butcher" by his American adversaries, had been ordered to capture Governor Jefferson and the members of Virginia's legislature. He sent a detachment led by Captain Kenneth McLeod to Monticello, where several of the Virginia lawmakers were staying.

Below Mount Alto, Charlottesville looked calm and quiet. The beating of hooves would signal an approaching cavalry. Jefferson heard none, so he raced back to the house. He hadn't gone more than a few feet when he realized that the light sword he was wearing had slipped out of its sheath. He found it close to where he had been kneeling. This gave him one more chance to check the activity in Charlottesville. Through his telescope, he saw the town swarming with white-and-green-uniformed British dragoons! There was no time to waste.

In fact, McCleod's men were already inside Jefferson's house, questioning his slaves about their master's whereabouts. Jefferson mounted his horse and rode off with minutes to spare.

As the author of the Declaration of Independence, Thomas Jefferson was one of the most wanted men in the 13 colonies. The words he had written were powerful. They had inspired people to fight for freedom. What had been considered a civil war—a war between Great Britain and its citizens in the colonies—had become a war of independence. The colonies had become a threat to the greater British Empire.

Those who orchestrated this rebellion, including Jefferson, George Washington, Benjamin Franklin, and John Adams, were now traitors to the British Crown. If any one of them was captured, the punishment would be torture and death.

With a wave of the pen, the signers of the Declaration of Independence put their lives in jeopardy for the freedom of the nation.

1

The Surveyor

Thomas Jefferson grew up in Virginia, a wild, sparsely inhabited place full of possibilities, in an age of new ideas. Isaac Newton had unlocked the secrets of motion and gravity, John Locke had declared that all men were born equal, and Denis Diderot was putting together the first encyclopedia to free ordinary people from ignorance. Although they originated in Europe, these ideas had crossed over to the New World.

The British colonies lined the east coast of North America, as shown in this 1755 map.

At the time of Thomas's birth, Virginia was one of 13 British colonies in North America. By the time he died, it was part of the United States of America. Enormous changes took place in between, and he was responsible for many of them. But the times made him as much as he made the times.

Back then, no one knew how far America stretched west;

most people were still loyal to the mother country, Great Britain; and colonists lived in varying degrees of peace with African slaves and American Indians. Settlements rose along the eastern seaboard, where wealthy colonists built manor houses and huge plantations with the help of slave labor.

Plenty of land was available for rugged, ambitious settlers like Thomas's father, Peter Jefferson, who was a successful surveyor. It was Peter who, with his friend Joshua Fry, drew the first map of Virginia for the king's geographer.

Thomas Jefferson fell in love with the Natural Bridge of Virginia, the "most sublime of Nature's works," and purchased the land on which it stood.

He brought home stories to his wide-eyed son of horses tumbling off cliffs and of crossing the "River Styx," where they lost supplies and faced near starvation.

Peter acquired a 1,400-acre tract of land just a few miles east of Charlottesville to establish a tobacco plantation. With the help of slaves, he built a one-and-a-half-story farmhouse. Peter named it Shadwell, after the London parish where his wife, Jane Randolph, was born.

Virginia Elite

Jane Randolph, Jefferson's mother, belonged to one of Virginia's most prominent families. It traced its noble bloodline back to England and Scotland and owned huge plantations that were worked by hundreds of slaves. The Randolphs are mentioned in Herman Melville's 1851 novel *Moby Dick*.

On April 13, 1743, Thomas was born at Shadwell. Peter and Jane already had two daughters, Jane and Mary. After Thomas, they had five more children: Elizabeth, Martha, and Lucy, and twins Anna and Randolph.

Growing up on the frontier of European settlement, Thomas loved the outdoors and developed a lifelong interest in natural history. Peter had gained the respect of the neighboring Cherokee Indians, who dropped by from time to time. In 1812, Thomas wrote that Indians were "a people with whom, in the early part of my life, I was very familiar . . . I knew much of the great Ontasseté, the warrior and orator of the Cherokees; he was always the guest of my father. . . . "

Thomas also grew up with slaves. His family owned a dozen slaves, including children, who were his playmates. He played with a boy his age named Jupiter, who would become his personal valet. With the shortage of European servants in the 1600s, tobacco farmers, who were concentrated in the South, started to rely on slaves brought from Africa. Tobacco was a labor-intensive crop, and a tobacco economy was impossible to sustain without a large contingent of workers. By the mid-1700s, slaves made up 40 percent of Virginia's population.

As a child, Thomas wasn't around Shadwell much. In 1746, when he was two years old, he moved with his family to nearby Tuckahoe, the former home of his mother's recently deceased cousin, William Randolph. Randolph, a widower, had asked Peter to look after his children and estate after his death.

Thomas started attending school with the three Randolph children at the age of five, but his black friends, the children of slaves, did not go with him. At the

Tobacco was the most important export crop in the American colonies. Here, slaves seal barrels of tobacco for shipment.

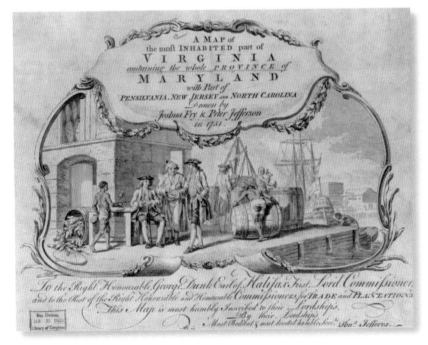

A MAP of the most INHABITED part of VIRGINIA containing the whole PROVINCE of MARYLAND with Part of PENSILVANIA, NEW JERSEY and NORTH CAROLINA Drawn by Joshua Fry & Peter Jefferson in 1751.

To the Right Honourable George Dunk Earl of Halifax, First Lord Commissioner, and to the Rest of the Right Honourable and Honourable Commissioners for TRADE and PLANTATIONS. This Map is most humbly Inscribed to their Lordships. By their Lordships Most Obedient & most devoted humble Servt. Thos. Jefferys.

time, it was considered unnatural to give slaves a serious education. His father taught the slaves carpentry, farming, and the other skills they needed to run the plantation.

The Jefferson family, which now included six children, moved back to Shadwell when Thomas was nine. Shortly afterward, he enrolled in the Latin School 50 miles (80 km) away. He boarded with Reverend William Douglas, the Scottish minister who ran the school. Thomas later recalled Douglas's "mouldy pies and excellent instruction."

Thomas returned to Shadwell—a two day journey by horse and carriage—during summers and holidays. While there, he learned from his father to be a skilled horseman, paddle a canoe, and hunt. He would eventually follow in his father's footsteps as a surveyor, farmer, and member of the Virginia House of Burgesses, the oldest legislature in the colonies. Peter, a self-taught man, told his son: "Never ask another to do for you what you can do for yourself."

Thomas took his father's lessons to heart. He didn't just come up with great ideas—he also put them to work. When he read a book, he did so in its original language—*Don Quixote* in Spanish and *The Iliad* in Greek. He studied the English Common Law in its original texts.

Peter also wanted Thomas to receive a classical education. So, after his father died in 1757, Thomas went to study at Reverend James Maury's Classical School for Boys. (Reverend Maury

COMMON LAW

Common law was a British system of laws based on precedent and custom.

would also teach two other future presidents, James Madison and James Monroe.) Inside the one-room schoolhouse, Thomas studied Greek and Roman literature, manners and morals, mathematics, literature, history and geography, as well as Latin, Greek, Italian, French, and Spanish.

Reverend Maury may have sown the seeds for Thomas's future endeavors in the unexplored West. He, along with Thomas's father, was a member of the Loyal Company, an organization dedicated to expanding Virginia's borders into the western frontier. This group knew the importance of the Missouri River as a path to westward expansion, and even planned an expedition to follow it all the way to the Pacific Ocean (though in fact it didn't extend that far).

During his two years at the Classical School, Thomas boarded with Reverend Maury's family. But as eldest son, he also had to care for his mother, six sisters, and baby brother, and he returned to Shadwell on weekends and in the summer to help.

After a long day's work, the Jefferson children would sing and play instruments together. Thomas's sister Jane played the harpsichord and encouraged him to accompany her on the violin. He called the violin "the favorite passion of my soul" and he would often practice three times a day.

One of Reverend Maury's other students, Dabney Carr, became Thomas's closest friend. Thomas and Dabney, sometimes accompanied by Thomas's sisters, would ride several miles to a mountain peak surrounded by woods. The two boys made a pact that whoever died first would be buried by the other beneath their favorite tree on "Tom's Mountain."

Thomas graduated from the Classical School for Boys, but his natural intelligence and habits wouldn't permit him to be idle. "It is wonderful how much may be done if we are always doing," he later wrote. Like other young men, Thomas was fond of concerts, dances, and the occasional card game. But he felt guilty that he wasn't more focused, and at the age of 16 wrote to his guardian that he wished to go to college. In that year, 1760, he entered the College of William and Mary in Williamsburg, Virginia. In the 18th century, the college included an Indian school, founded to educate and "Christianize" Indian boys. Eight Indian students attended William and Mary at the same time as Thomas.

The College of William and Mary, named after English monarchs, was located in Virginia's colonial capital of Williamsburg.

On the way to his first year of college, Thomas spent the Christmas holidays feasting and dancing at the

home of Colonel Nathan Dandridge. It was there that Thomas met Patrick Henry, a future advocate of independence, who inspired him to pursue law and politics.

The Flat Hat club

While at the College of William and Mary, Jefferson joined a secret society called the Flat Hat Club, or "F.H.C." It was the precursor to the academic honor society Phi Beta Kappa. Jefferson said the club served no useful purpose.

Thomas was accompanied to school by Jupiter, his valet and childhood friend. Jupiter was in charge of Thomas's personal affairs: shaving and dressing him; buying hair powder, buckles, and theater tickets. He would later also carry out important errands such as paying bills and delivering documents to the legislature.

In Williamsburg, Thomas's well-connected relatives took him under their wing, introducing him to elegant society. He spent more of his first year socializing, riding horses,

Young Jefferson dined at the Governor's Palace in Williamsburg, and later moved in as governor himself.

and playing the violin than his conscience could accept. So he wrote to his guardian asking that his first year's college expenses be deducted from his inheritance. He was answered: "No—if you have sowed your wild oats thus, the estate can well afford to pay the bill!"

Thomas Jefferson met his destiny with a combination of hard work and luck. During his second year at William and Mary, he studied up to 15 hours a day, and finished college at the end of that year. He also acquired three invaluable mentors.

The first, Dr. William Small, was professor of philosophy at William and Mary. Dr. Small introduced Jefferson to the scientific method and to the greatest minds of the previous two centuries: Francis Bacon, Thomas Hobbes, Jean-Jacques Rousseau, John Locke, Isaac Newton, and others. He was happy to spend his free time with such a bright and eager student. In his memoirs, Jefferson would write that Dr. Small "probably fixed the destinies of my life."

JURIST

A jurist is a judge or legal scholar.

Dr. Small returned to Britain in 1764, but not before introducing Jefferson to George Wythe. Jefferson had decided to stay in Williamsburg to study law, and Wythe, a prominent attorney, judge, and law professor, took him as a student. He assigned him the books of the famed jurist Sir Edward Coke, who was the final word on English common law. Jefferson considered Wythe to be a second father.

In turn, Wythe introduced Jefferson to the governor of Virginia, Francis Fauquier. Thomas met regularly with Small, Wythe, and Fauquier at the governor's palace for dinner and stimulating conversation. From these meetings, he gained a heightened appreciation of the arts, fine wines, music, politics, philosophy, and science. He also acquired a "polish of manner which distinguished him through life" during his time with "the elegant society which Governor Fauquier collected about him," according to his 19th century biographer Henry S. Randall.

At age 22, Jefferson was also starting to enjoy the attention of the opposite sex.

Jefferson learned the law from George Wythe, who was one of the signers of the Declaration of Independence.

He was six foot two (188 cm), physically fit, with deep-set hazel eyes, and chestnut-red hair. At a dance at the Raleigh Tavern, he became infatuated with 16-year-old Rebecca Burwell. But the courtship didn't go well, and she ultimately married someone else.

Jefferson didn't brood. Instead, he turned his attention to a practical matter affecting his family's plantation. At the time, the tobacco that his family grew had to be transported to Richmond by land, which was a slow and expensive job. Although the Rivanna River flowed nearby, treacherous boulders made it impossible for larger vessels to navigate.

Jefferson was determined to find a way to use the river for transportation. He explored the Rivanna by canoe and discovered that the rocks blocking his passage could be dislodged. Soon he had raised enough money to clear a channel through which harvests could be transported on rafts. This successful project would later inspire his grander schemes for the Mississippi River.

Jefferson had good reason to apply his intelligence to the business of farming. When he turned 21, he had become a landowner. He had inherited 2,750 acres of his father's land—not including Shadwell, which remained his mother's property—plus about 30 slaves. At the time there was a lot for a landowner and tobacco farmer to worry about. The tobacco-based economy of the colonies was in decline after the Seven Years' War, and ordinary people protested the ever-increasing taxes. The war had cost the British government a great deal of money, and somehow, it had to be financed. The British people, already paying their own skyrocketing taxes, looked to the colonies for revenue. For one thing, they wanted Americans to make good on the debts they owed from buying British goods. For another, they felt that the colonies benefited most from the war: Britain had protected its colonies from the encroaching French, and many thought the colonists should pay their fair share.

H.R.H. George III

Under King George III, the British Empire was the world's dominant colonial power. Although he was not responsible for the policies, such as the Stamp Act of 1765, that led to American rebellion, Thomas Jefferson directed his ire in the Declaration of Independence at King George. He wasn't hated by all colonists. For most Loyalists, he was a hero.

It was George Wythe's idea that his young protégé attend the courts when they were in session, to listen and learn. What Jefferson observed was that the country was heading toward separation from Britain. His friend, Patrick Henry, whom Governor Fauquier once referred to as young and hotheaded, stood before the House of Burgesses and argued openly for defiance of Britain.

chapter 2

Listening at the Wall

Patrick Henry was already known as a firebrand in April 1765, when word reached Williamsburg of the latest tax from the British Parliament. It was yet another in a series of taxes designed to extract more money from the colonies.

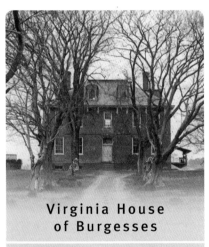

Virginia House of Burgesses

The Virginia House of Burgesses, established in 1619, was the first elected legislative assembly in the 13 colonies. It was there that many of the leaders of the Revolutionary War made their names. In 1776, it was transformed into the Virginia House of Delegates.

At the entrance to the assembly chamber, Jefferson quietly observed as debates raged over the Stamp Act. Starting in November, special stamps would be required on newspapers, marriage licenses, brochures, diplomas, and even playing cards, showing that tax had been paid. The taxes went to England, in part to support a force of 10,000 redcoats stationed througout the vast territories acquired after the Seven Years' War.

A redcoat was a British soldier in the 17th to 19th centuries, whose uniform included a red coat.

Patrick Henry argued against the Stamp Act before the House of Burgesses. He insisted that in accordance with British law, Virginia had the right to be taxed only by its own representatives. This was the first official challenge to the rule of Britain over the colonies, and the speech was interrupted by cries of "Treason!" Nevertheless, four of Henry's seven resolutions were adopted—including one that authorized taxation only by the people themselves or their chosen representatives, which he called "the only security against a burdensome taxation."

Throughout the colonies, ordinary people also expressed their objections to the Stamp Act. They protested in the street, destroyed property, and attacked the homes of royal governors. The Stamp Act was repealed on March 17, 1766, but by then, the die was cast.

Late in 1765, Jefferson's younger sister Martha married his best friend, Dabney Carr. But this happy news was followed by tragedy when his

The citizens of Boston protested the Stamp Act by burning a British representative in effigy and ransacking his house.

beloved sister Jane died at the age of just 25. In grief, Jefferson turned to his work. The following year, he left Virginia for the first time and took a tour of Annapolis, Philadelphia, and New York, where there was rejoicing over the repeal of the Stamp Act. He traveled on horseback, so it took him several days to go from town to town.

At the age of 24, Jefferson began practicing law and had immediate success. In court, his style was mild and reflective, the opposite of the emotional intensity of his friend Patrick Henry. But it was hard to get rich on a lawyer's income. Even though he earned an average of £370 a year (about $60,000 in today's money), his clients often failed to pay. Soon, he began to turn his attention elsewhere. But even after giving up his practice eight years later, his activities as a statesman would reflect his legal training.

Jefferson was elected to the Virginia House of Burgesses the following year—just in time for a new wave of colonial rebellion.

The British Crown had long regarded the colonies as a source of raw materials, such as silk, lumber, leather, corn, and rice, and a ready buyer of British exports such as cloth, furniture, weapons, sugar, and tea. Over the years, the king had paid little attention to his colonial subjects, who in turn got in the habit of doing things their own way. Colonists began to think of themselves as Virginians, New Englanders, and so forth, as much as Englishmen.

Meanwhile, Britain still needed to raise £40,000. But the colonists had already shown that they were violently opposed to internal taxes. What could Parliament do to raise the money it needed? Charles Townshend, chancellor of the exchequer, had the answer: external taxes, payable at American ports.

Colonists made their own homespun cloth rather than importing fabrics from overseas.

Parliament passed the Townshend Acts of Trade and Revenue, which imposed a small import duty on glass, paint, paper, lead, and tea.

The colonists weren't so easily fooled. Thomas and the other Virginia lawmakers considered these Acts to be a direct threat to the colonial governments. They resolved that Virginia should no longer submit to parliamentary taxation and would no longer send criminals to England for trial. There may have been some self-interest in this last point— after all, those who voted for these treasonous resolutions would have been among those criminals!

The new royal governor dissolved the House of Burgesses less than two weeks after Jefferson was sworn in. So members of the assembly met up at the Raleigh Tavern instead. Jefferson and his colleagues called for a boycott of products imported from England. Patriot women

PATRIOT

A patriot was someone who supported the rights of the colonies during the American Revolution.

The English philosopher John Locke argued that it was reasonable to revolt against tyrannical governments.

did their part by picking up lost skills like spinning and weaving. They dressed in "homespun" or "Virginia cloth" instead of the beautiful silks and laces they had once imported from England. Many gave up drinking tea. Parliament gave in by removing the Townshend Acts, except for the tax on tea.

In the midst of these escalating tensions, Jefferson did a bold thing: He made his first attempt to curtail slavery. He knew that the institution of slavery couldn't be abolished in a single stroke, so he took a small step. He proposed a law making it legal for a slave owner to free a slave.

Jefferson's thoughts on human rights owe a debt to the English philosopher, John Locke. Locke wrote that human beings were naturally rational, tolerant, and happy. He believed that the only reason for the existence of government was to protect their natural rights to "life, liberty, and estate [property]." Jefferson later borrowed this phrase for the Declaration of Independence, changing it to "life, liberty, and the pursuit of happiness." Now he applied these principles to his bill, but it was rejected. The issue of slavery was set aside for more pressing matters.

Like many of his contemporaries, Jefferson himself was a slave owner. By 1776, he owned 117 slaves. Monticello was a 5,000-acre plantation that required a lot of attention. There was a smokehouse, a blacksmith's shop, a carpenter's shop, and a dairy. There was work for the slaves to do all year. Still, Jefferson looked for other ways. In 1774, he formed a company to produce olive oil and wine using paid labor instead of slaves. George Washington and Lord Dunmore, the royal governor of Virginia, were shareholders.

Jefferson may not have formally educated his slaves, but he didn't prevent them from learning to read and write, like most slave owners in Virginia did. In 1784, he proposed a public education system for slaves, but the measure never made it to law. Jefferson freed two of his slaves during his lifetime and five in his will, including his butler, Burwell Colbert. It's easy for modern readers to condemn Jefferson for owning slaves while preaching freedom, but for the times in which he lived, his actions were very forward-thinking.

In any case, in the late 1760s, Jefferson's grand estate was still just a dream. As a self-taught architect, he studied drawings of Italian buildings in the planning of his new home. He named it Monticello, Italian for

The Enlightenment

The Enlightenment was an important period in Western philosophy, roughly corresponding with the 18th century. During this time, great thinkers such as Voltaire, John Locke, Thomas Hume, and Jean-Jacques Rousseau questioned many traditional ideas.

"Architecture is among the most important arts," said Jefferson, who drew this plan for the front of Monticello.

"little mountain." In 1768, he began clearing and leveling a site atop a 850-foot (260-m) mountain near Charlottesville—and not a moment too soon. A fire burned down the main house at Shadwell on February 1, 1770, destroying the Jefferson family's important papers and, worse, their collection of books. Fortunately, no one was hurt, and a slave managed to save Jefferson's fiddle.

Jefferson moved into rented rooms in Charlottesville while his mother and sisters lived in the outbuildings of Shadwell. By November 1770, he had completed a two-room cottage at Monticello with the help of his slaves and hired workers.

Jefferson spent the following year laying out plans for expanding Monticello, perhaps hoping to find a wife. In Williamsburg, he met a pretty, intelligent 23-year-old widow named Martha Wayles Skelton. Jefferson called her Patty. They married on New Year's Day 1772, and Jefferson looked forward to a quiet life of domestic tranquility. That fall, their first baby, Martha, or "Patsy," was born.

Martha had a great deal of responsibility at Monticello. She supervised food preparation and preservation. She was in charge of making soap and candles, planting vegetables, and overseeing the slaughter of livestock for consumption and for sale. She kept detailed records in an accounts book.

Monticello was host to many distinguished visitors over the years. Since travel in those days was difficult and slow, guests often stayed for weeks at a time. It was up to Martha to see to their comfort and entertainment. This was a happy period and perhaps the longest that the couple spent together. With revolution brewing, Jefferson was called away from home again.

On the night of March 4, 1773, five men filed into the white building that was the Raleigh Tavern. Above the front entrance, the lead bust of Sir Walter Raleigh, who attempted to colonize Virginia in 1585, impassively watched the unfolding scene. The men passed the dining room and the gaming room and made their way to the Apollo Room, where they could speak in private. They were Thomas Jefferson, Patrick Henry, Richard Henry Lee, Francis Lightfoot Lee, and Dabney Carr. (There may have been one or two others present, but later in life, Jefferson didn't remember them.)

There was much to discuss. The summer before, the

Jefferson was one of a handful of men who met at the Raleigh Tavern to discuss the fate of America.

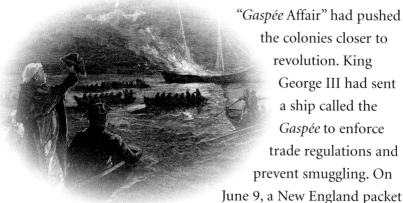

"*Gaspée* Affair" had pushed the colonies closer to revolution. King George III had sent a ship called the *Gaspée* to enforce trade regulations and prevent smuggling. On June 9, a New England packet sloop, the *Hannah*, lured the *Gaspée* into shallow waters. Run aground, the *Gaspée* was then boarded by Patriots from eight longboats. They took Lieutenant William Dudingston and his crew prisoner. Then they set fire to the ship, causing the powder magazine to explode.

Angry colonists in Rhode Island capture the crew of the HMS *Gaspée* and set it on fire.

The incident drew attention to the British law that permitted those charged with treason to be sent to England for trial. Although there wasn't enough evidence to convict the Patriots who burned the *Gaspée*, the Burgesses were alarmed by such a threat to their "ancient, legal, and constitutional rights." Something had to be done. Jefferson and his colleagues agreed that night on a standing Committee of Correspondence to help open the discussion to all the colonies.

In those days, handwritten letters were delivered on horseback or ships. It could take months for a letter to reach its recipient. During times of crisis, colonial legislatures sometimes used a committee system to make communications more efficient. The Committee of Correspondence of one colony agreed on certain resolutions and sent letters to inform similar groups in the other colonies. This way, good information was communicated securely. However, previous committees had been temporary; once a crisis was over, they were disbanded.

Smuggling

Smuggling was a normal part of international trade in the 17th and 18th centuries. It increased whenever Britain passed import taxes. One method of smuggling was to declare only part of one's cargo. For example, a merchant would pay taxes only on cheap teas, while hiding better ones. From the mid-18th century, smugglers imported up to 900,000 pounds of cheap foreign tea a year.

The resolutions approved on March 12 by the House of Burgesses (which had been reformed) called for a permanent Committee of Correspondence. Soon, every colony had a standing committee. Next on the agenda was to set up a united congress that would meet annually.

Three months after the fateful meeting at the Raleigh Tavern, Dabney Carr died of typhoid fever. Jefferson remembered his promise to bury his friend beneath their favorite oak tree on "Tom's Mountain." Unfortunately, he was away at the time of his friend's death, and Carr was buried at Shadwell. To honor his promise, Jefferson had the body moved. He also brought his widowed sister, Martha Jefferson

CONGRESS

A congress is a formal meeting of representatives for the purpose of making laws.

Carr, and her six children to live at Monticello, even though there was very little room in the house at the time.

Two weeks later, Jefferson's father-in-law, John Wayles, died. From Wayles, Jefferson inherited 135 slaves, in addition to £4000 in debts. It was difficult and expensive to run one plantation, and Jefferson's property had grown overnight to include several plantations in Albemarle, as well as the Poplar Forest estate, 90 miles (145 km) south of Monticello. He tried to pay off the debts by selling the land, but he accepted Virginia wartime currency, which was soon without value. (His creditors demanded payment in gold or sterling.)

Among the slaves he inherited was Elizabeth Hemings, known as Betty, and her family. It is thought that Wayles

Slaves may have sat at a desk like this one at Montcello when corresponding with Jefferson.

had fathered at least six of her twelve children, making them the half-brothers and half-sisters of Martha Wayles Jefferson. More than 75 of Betty Hemings's children, grandchildren, and great-grandchildren lived as slaves at Monticello.

Joseph Fossett

Joseph Fossett was one of the slaves Jefferson freed in his will. Fossett was a blacksmith and was married to Edith Hern, Jefferson's cook. After he was freed, he bought a shop in Charlottesville, and was able to free his wife and several of his children and grandchildren.

The slaves lived and worked on Mulberry Row, a 1,000-foot (305-m) road, south of the main house. Along the road were log dwellings, storage buildings, a stable, a smokehouse that doubled as a dairy, a sawmill, and a factory for making cloth. The cloth was used to make clothing for the slaves, but was also sold for profit.

Since Jefferson was away from Monticello for long periods, he hired overseers to manage his affairs. Some of his overseers were white men; some were free blacks. Jefferson kept in touch with his overseers by letters.

"No servants ever had a kinder master than Mr. Jefferson's," wrote Edmund Bacon, one of Jefferson's white overseers. "He did not like slavery. I have heard him talk a great deal about it. He thought it a bad system."

"No servants ever had a kinder master than Mr. Jefferson's…"

–Edmund Bacon, Monticello overseer

chapter 3

The Farmer Revolutionary

Parliament assumed that the colonists would rather pay a small tax than give up the pleasure of a cup of tea, so it allowed the Tea Act to remain even after the Townshend Acts were repealed. The colonists continued to boycott tea—if they paid the tax, they acknowledged the right of the Crown to tax them. Furthermore, Parliament gave the British East India Company a monopoly to import tea to America. This made it less expensive for colonists to buy tea, but only through official channels. No one was happy about this, least of all the colonial merchants who would be excluded from the tea trade.

> **MONOPOLY**
>
> In a monopoly, one seller has control of the entire market.

British East India Company

The British East India Company was formed in 1600 to help British merchants trade in the East Indies, which included India and the Middle East. The company had its own army and set up forts in its eastern colonies. By the mid-19th century, one-fifth of the world's population was under British rule thanks to the company's trade dominance.

In protest, the colonists refused to allow British vessels carrying shipments of tea to dock. They went as far as to drink locally grown tea (which must have taken some getting used to after drinking the fragrant teas imported from India).

Angry colonists boarded three ships and threw 90,000 pounds (41,000 kg) of tea into Boston Harbor.

In the winter of 1773, three ships belonging to the East India Company docked in Boston Harbor. They were the *Eleanor*, the *Dartmouth*, and the *Beaver*. Some 7,000 agitated locals milled about the wharf, refusing to allow the ships to unload their cargo. British warships pointed their cannons at the wharf, ready to fire if the Americans continued to block the shipments.

Patriot Samuel Adams organized the famous protest that is known as the Boston Tea Party. On December 16, dozens of men boarded the three ships, and in the following hours axed open 342 wooden chests and threw 90,000 pounds (41,000 kg) of tea into the harbor. The men had painted their faces with coal dust from a blacksmith, in the manner of Indian warriors, and armed themselves with tomahawks and clubs to complete the illusion that they were a band of Indians. The crowd on the wharf watched everything beneath the light of the moon.

Surprisingly, no attempt was made to stop or arrest the Patriot raiders. After the deed was done, they returned to

> *"An attack on any one colony ... [is] an attack on the whole."*
>
> –Thomas Jefferson

their homes. Their identities remain a mystery to this day.

Parliament responded to the Boston Tea Party by passing several acts, which became known in the colonies as the Intolerable Acts. One of these, the Boston Port Bill, ordered that Boston Harbor be closed until the ruined tea was paid for. This led to widespread unemployment and hunger.

Express riders from the Boston Committee of Correspondence delivered the news of the port closure to the Virginia Assembly, asking for help. The younger burgesses were determined to take a stand. The older ones, including George Wythe, were afraid of rapid change and preferred to let things calm down. Jefferson and the others were frustrated by the older men's lack of leadership.

Once again, Jefferson, Patrick Henry, Richard Henry Lee, and Francis Lightfoot Lee met at the Raleigh Tavern. They agreed that "an attack on any one colony, should be considered as an attack on the whole." Jefferson also proposed a day of fasting and prayer on the day the port of Boston was scheduled to be closed.

The next step was to discuss a united response to Great Britain. The Continental Congress called for a convention to do just that. On September 5, 1774, delegates from

CONVENTION

A convention is a large, formal assembly.

every colony but Georgia (whose governor was loyal to the king) convened at Carpenter's Hall in Philadelphia.

Jefferson returned to Monticello to supervise the farming of his fields, and to draft instructions for the Virginia delegates. He wanted to remind George III that "kings are the servants, not the proprietors of the people" and that "the god who gave us life, gave us liberty at the same time." He hoped the king would take steps to "quiet the minds of your subjects in British America" which would "establish fraternal love and harmony thro' the whole empire."

Jefferson was on his way to Williamsburg with the instructions in hand, when he devloped dystentery (an infection of the digestive system) and had to turn around.

"All my wishes end, where I hope my days end, at Monticello," said Jefferson, whose home and farm were a refuge from public life.

But he sent Jupiter to deliver

Common Sense

Founding Father Thomas Paine argued for the Revolutionary War in his 1776 pamphlet, *Common Sense*. It was written like a sermon, referring to government as nothing more than "a necessary evil" and stating that the "blood of the slain" called for separation between Britain and the colonies. Surprisingly, he had migrated to the colonies from England only two years earlier.

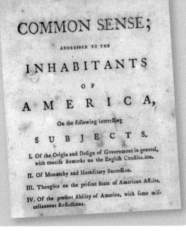

one copy of his instructions to burgesses Patrick Henry and Peyton Randolph. Unfortunately, because of his illness, Jefferson could not be elected as a delegate himself.

Congress remained in session from September 5 until October 26. Although the idea was to present a united front against Britain, in fact each colony had very different goals. One half wanted to be treated equally and fairly under British rule, and the other half wanted to be separated from Great Britain entirely. In the end, Congress voted to hold another session in a year if Britain did nothing to ease colonial grievances.

Jefferson's suggestions for a formal letter to George III were not adopted, but his ideas struck a chord. Patrick Henry announced: "I am not a Virginian, but an American." Congress called for a declaration of rights to be written, and agreed that Americans would stop trade with Great Britain.

In his absence, Jefferson's friends printed his notes under the title *A Summary View of the Rights of British America*. When copies reached England, Jefferson's name was added to a list of traitors to the Crown.

"Give me liberty or give me death!"

–Patrick Henry

In May 1775, Virginia lawmakers received the shocking news that on April 18, British redcoats and Massachusetts militiamen (citizen soldiers) had exchanged shots at the towns of Lexington and Concord. The British had fired on the American militia, which was assembled on the Lexington Common, shouting, "Dispense, ye rebels!"

Jefferson wrote to his beloved teacher William Small that "this accident has cut off our last hopes of reconciliation." Depending on where you stood, Britain and the colonies were now caught up in a civil war or a war of independence. The colonists wanted liberty or death, in the words of Patrick Henry. Congress immediately urged the colonies to begin writing their own state constitutions, laying the groundwork for them to become independent states.

In mid-June, Jefferson, accompanied by Jupiter, traveled for 10 days by carriage to attend the Second Continental Congress. There were no bridges over the rivers from Williamsburg to Philadelphia, and the roads were muddy and pitted. By the time he arrived,

CONSTITUTION

A constitution is a document establishing the structure, procedures, powers, and duties of a government.

Jefferson admired John Adams, but political differences created a rift between them.

Congress had already been in session for several weeks.

At age 32, Jefferson was one of the youngest delegates. But he arrived with the reputation of being a gifted writer, since many of the other delegates had read and admired his *Summary View of the Rights of British America*. There was mutual admiration when Jefferson met John Adams, a lawyer from Massachusetts who was a driving force for independence, and the renowned philosopher and senior statesman Benjamin Franklin.

John Adams and his radical followers believed that war was inevitable. But as late as July 5, 1775, Congress sent a final appeal, known as the Olive Branch Petition, to George III, asking him to redress colonial grievances and avoid war.

However, any thoughts of reconciliation were in vain after the Battles of Lexington and Concord, which had drawn thousands of rebels from around New England to Boston, in order to surround the British redcoats garrisoned there. It seemed that war was inevitable.

Congress had established an American army—but only on paper. The rebels gathered around Boston would have to be adopted into the new Continental Army. George Washington, who had distinguished himself in the French and Indian War, was in charge, but he had not yet joined his soldiers.

Meanwhile, the rebels—mostly farmers, fishermen, and merchants—trapped the redcoats inside Boston. The militia moved to fortify the peninsula. The soldiers were headed to Bunker Hill in nearby Charlestown, but American Colonel William Prescott changed his mind and dug into Breed's Hill, closer to Boston. His men took their positions, then fired and reloaded again and again. The fighting lasted all day.

The redcoats pursued the rebels as far as Bunker Hill, on June 17. To conserve ammunition, Prescott instructed his soldiers: "Don't fire until you see the whites of their eyes!" In spite of this, the militia ran out of ammunition and had to resort to close combat with bayonets and fists. There were many desertions.

The conflict at Bunker Hill had been the decisive battle in a larger siege of Boston by the British. Finally, the redcoats gained control of Breed's Hill and the entire area, but they had suffered huge casualties in the process. This was the bloodiest battle in the Revolutionary War.

Jefferson returned to Monticello in September. Soon

Minutemen were the elite of the colonial militia. Their readiness and marksmanship helped win the day at Concord.

after, his second daughter, Jane, died. She was only 17 months old. Martha was devastated, and Jefferson extended his visit to care for her. Eventually, he had to return to Congress, so he sent Martha and three-year-old Patsy to stay with Martha's half-sister, Elizabeth Eppes.

On New Year's Day 1776, Jefferson's home colony of Virginia joined the fighting when Britain's Lord Dunmore led an attack on Norfolk. Then on March 31, 1776, Jefferson's mother died at the age of 57. Soon after, he developed a migraine headache that would recur for the rest of his days.

When Jefferson returned to Congress on May 14, a month-old letter from his old friend John Page awaited him. It said: "For God's sake declare the colonies independent and save us from ruin." Jefferson started work on a constitution for his home state. In it he developed ideas, including a list of grievances against the king, that would appear in his work on the Declaration of Independence. But George Mason, a Fairfax County farmer who was a close friend of Washington's, beat him to the punch, with the Virginia Declaration of Rights.

Jefferson wasn't bothered by being upstaged. He was more worried about Martha, who hadn't written to him in a while.

He wanted to go home, but the Virginia delegation needed him in Philadelphia.

On June 1, Richard Henry Lee of the Virginia delegation proposed this resolution:

> That these United Colonies are & of right ought to be free & independent states, that they are absolved from all allegiance to the British crown, and that all political connection between them & the state of Great Britain is & ought to be, totally dissolved.

Some delegates were reluctant to support it because they still held the belief that kings were chosen by God and answerable only to him. This was the kind of thinking that still divided families and friends throughout the colonies, and which Jefferson, guided by the political and philosophical ideas of the Enlightenment, fought against.

Because the delegates knew Jefferson was a fine writer and scholar, they asked him to write the declaration. For 17 days, he stayed in his rented rooms in a quiet brick house, composing the hauntingly beautiful words that began:

> We hold these truths to be self-evident, that all men are created equal, that they are endowed by their Creator with inherent and

Wartime Communications

The war was good and bad news for journalism. There were six more newspapers in America after the war than before, for a total of 43, but most of them interrupted publication at some time during the years of conflict. Mail service was worse than ever.

inalienable rights, that among these are life, liberty, and the pursuit of Happiness.

The Declaration of Independence was necessary to explain to the world why the colonies were separating from Britain, and to put America on an even platform with other countries. These were not just 13 colonies rebelling from the Crown, but a nation fighting for its freedom. Jefferson hoped his words would inspire Americans to take action and fight.

Jefferson presented a draft of the declaration to Congress on Friday, June 28. It was just one of many items Congress had to review. The following Monday was July 1, the deadline for the delegates to vote on Richard Henry Lee's resolutions that the colonies were free and independent states. Deliberations were slow. The delegates took their time because everyone knew that a vote for independence was a vote for war. The signers of a declaration of independence would be considered traitors. Nevertheless, on July 2, the Continental Congress voted in favor of Lee's resolution for independence.

Jefferson finished writing a draft of the Declaration of Independence in 17 days. He then passed it to John Adams and Benjamin Franklin, who made slight changes.

By the time Jefferson met him, Benjamin Franklin was already famous as a scientist, inventor, printer, and diplomat. He was also a vegetarian.

John Adams wrote to his wife: "The second day of July, 1776, will be the most memorable epoch in the History of America. I am apt to believe that it will be celebrated by Succeeding generations as the great anniversary festival." (He was two days off. We celebrate the Fourth of July because it was on that day that the Declaration was adopted.)

Once the resolution had been approved, Jefferson's draft was dissected and criticized. He was irritated because Congress removed the clause that condemned slavery, at the insistence of Georgia and South Carolina, whose plantation economies depended on slave labor. But finally, on July 15, it became "the Unanimous Declaration of the Thirteen United States of America." The document was printed immediately and distributed to the states for proclamation. There would be no turning back.

At the signing of the Declaration, John Hancock is said to have told Benjamin Franklin that the delegates would all hang together. Franklin replied: "Yes, we must indeed all hang together, or else, most assuredly we shall all hang separately."

chapter **4**

Fight for Freedom

In August 1776, the same month that the Declaration of Independence was signed, the British were back in full force, fighting the still-green Continental Army on Long Island, New York.

Jefferson, always delighted by inventions, must have heard of the submarine that was launched against British ships in New York Harbor. The "Turtle" failed in its mission to plant a keg of explosive powder in the hull of the Royal Navy's flagship, HMS *Eagle*, but it was an impressive craft.

Martha Jefferson was unwell, and wrote to beg her husband to return home. He agreed. His visit did her good, and her health improved enough for her to accompany him to Williamsburg that fall for a meeting of Virginia's General Assembly.

Over the next two years, Martha gave birth to two babies: a son who only lived for 17 days, and

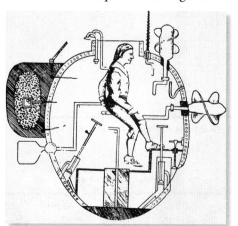

The "Turtle," so named because of its appearance, was the first submarine to attack an enemy warship.

wrote: "The public would have more confidence in a military chief." Washington sent the French Marquis de Lafayette with 1,200 soldiers, beginning a lifelong friendship between Jefferson and Lafayette.

Gilbert du Motier, the Marquis de Lafayette, sailed to America at age 19 to help the revolutionaries fight.

The General Assembly moved once again, this time to Charlottesville, near Monticello, where the governor was passing the last few days of his second term. Forty miles (64 km) away was a place called the Cuckoo Tavern. It was there, on June 3, 1781, that a Patriot named Jack Jouett was woken by a stampede of horses and the rattle of swords.

The horses belonged to Lieutenant Colonel Banastre Tarleton and his dragoons—the same soldiers who had dealt several bloody defeats to the Americans in North and South Carolina.

Watching Tarleton and his cavalry, Jouett quickly deduced their objective: to capture the rebels, including Jefferson, Patrick Henry, and Richard Henry Lee, at Charlottesville. In order to warn them, Jouett would have to ride the distance on horseback in the dark of night and through

DRAGOONS

A dragoon rides horseback but fights on foot. The King's Dragoon Guard was a regiment in the British Army.

tangled backwoods to avoid being caught. That's exactly what he did. Jouett was whipped until bloody by the tree branches.

At dawn, he arrived at Monticello, waking Jefferson and the Virginia lawmakers who were his guests. He then got back on his horse and rode on to Charlottesville to warn the other legislators.

Jefferson made sure his guests were safe, and sent his family, escorted by Jupiter and another slave, to Enniscorthy, a friend's home about 14 miles (23 km) away. Then he went to the hilltop to look down on Charlottesville through his telescope. By the time he spotted Tarleton's dragoons, a detachment led by Captain Kenneth McLeod was inside Monticello. Jefferson jumped on his stallion Caractacus and rode away.

British Colonel Banastre Tarleton gained a reputation for ruthlessness at the Waxhaw Massacre in South Carolina, in which 113 Americans were killed.

Tarleton captured seven of the legislators as well as legendary frontiersman Daniel Boone, who was on his way to Charlottesville to take a seat in the assembly. Boone was released several days later.

Finally, things started to look up for the Americans. By July 1781, General Cornwallis was in Yorktown, Virginia, but his forces had been sapped by battles in the

Carolinas. The Americans and the French marched to confront him. On October 19, Cornwallis surrendered his 7,000-strong force to General Washington and the French commander, Rochambeau. The war was effectively over. Although the British still occupied many American cities and fighting continued, the war-weary Americans began to celebrate their inevitable victory.

Daniel Boone

The 1784 publication of *The Adventures of Colonel Daniel Boone* made the pioneer an American legend. The book describes his exploits facing hostile Indians in the Kentucky wilderness, beyond the borders of the 13 colonies. Jefferson may have crossed paths with Boone when he was a member of the Virginia legislature, after Kentucky was divided into three Virginia counties in 1780.

Meanwhile, Jefferson faced a personal crisis. The Virginia House passed a resolution calling for an inquiry into his conduct as governor. It questioned whether he had adequately prepared Virginia for the British invasion. The government had been chased out of Richmond in January and then out of Charlottesville in May. Many thought Jefferson should have stayed behind and fought back.

He was blamed for his restraint in the use of his authority as governor. When Lafayette requested reinforcements for his small detachment, Governor Jefferson declined because

> *"There never was a good war, or a bad peace."*
>
> –Benjamin Franklin, 1783

technically it wasn't in his power. As a result, the British chased Lafayette northward.

The General Assembly unanimously absolved Jefferson of all charges, but the episode left him humiliated and bitter. He resolved never to return to public life, and, suspecting that Patrick Henry was behind the charges against him, he cut off all ties with his former friend.

During the inquiry, Jefferson and his family remained in seclusion at his retreat at Poplar Forest. They stayed at an overseer's house, because he had not yet built his residence there. While there, Jefferson began drafting his *Notes on the State of Virginia,* a detailed reply to a French diplomat who had sent him a list of queries about his state.

Monticello, a three-day carriage ride away, was still recovering from the wreckage of the British invasion. Tarleton's men had consumed or destroyed a great deal of Jefferson's property, including horses, cattle, sheep, hogs, corn, tobacco, barley, and wheat. The animals that were left behind had their throats cut. Jefferson counted 27 slaves who had been taken away by the British. A few of the slaves were stricken with smallpox and made their way back to Monticello to die, spreading the disease to those who took care of them.

Around this time, news was spreading that the British Parliament had voted to end the war in America. On September 3, 1783, the colonies gained their hard-fought independence with the signing of Treaty of Paris between Britain and the United States. The country was celebrating its victory, but Jefferson, overworked and exhausted, felt only the burden of his personal trials.

Back at Monticello, Martha's health was failing, especially after the birth of the Jeffersons' last daughter in May. She was named Lucy Elizabeth after the baby they had lost, but the family simply called her Lu. Jefferson stayed by Martha's bedside for four months, taking only short breaks. On the day she died, she allowed some of the house servants who were closest to her to see her. They witnessed Martha telling her husband that one of the things she feared most was for her children to be raised by a stepmother as she had been. She made him promise never to remarry, and he never did.

Jefferson's beloved wife died at the age of 33. She had been a fragile woman who suffered many difficult pregnancies and the deaths of several of her children. Jefferson was distraught. He described their marriage as ten years of "unchequered happiness." In an age lacking the resources of modern medicine, many people died early. Of the Jeffersons' six children only two, Patsy and Polly, lived to adulthood.

As usual, Jefferson mourned his loss by getting back to work. He continued his *Notes on the State of Virginia*, the only book by Jefferson published in his lifetime. It contained his vision of a system of publicly funded schools in Virginia.

It was a blessing when Congress offered him a commission as trade minister to France.

chapter **5**

Jefferson in Paris

Jefferson's assignment to Paris was delayed when the ship that was supposed to take him there was stuck in the frozen Chesapeake Bay. He was back in Monticello when he received word that he had again been elected to Congress.

In Philadelphia, Jefferson and the other delegates faced a wide range of issues. How was the Continental Army to be disbanded? What was to be done with the large debts owed by each state and the foreign debts owed by the republic? How were territories won from the British to be governed? These questions would test the new nation for years.

Of the 31 state papers that Jefferson drafted in Congress, two were of lasting importance. The first was a proposal to replace the English monetary system of pounds, shillings, pence, and farthings with a decimal system based on the Spanish dollar. It led to the adoption of the dollar in 1792 as the basic monetary unit in the United States.

The second was his "Plan of Government for the Western Territory." Under the Treaty of Paris, Britain had ceded the Northwest Territory to the United States. This included land that would become Ohio, Indiana, Illinois, Wisconsin, and Michigan, and nearly doubled the size of the new nation. Virginia, Connecticut, New York, and Massachusetts had competing claims to the as-yet-unsettled territory. Jefferson called for the states to relinquish their claims, allowing the nation to expand through establishing new states rather than extending existing ones. A territory could become a new state once its population reached 60,000.

Jefferson envisioned 14 states with names such as Polypotamia and Chersonesus, after Native American and classical sources. Congress didn't care for most of them, but accepted Washington and forms of Michigania and Illinoia.

Jefferson also proposed that after the year 1800, there would be no slavery in the new states. The measure was defeated by one vote. This was not altogether surprising—southern economies still relied on slavery, and even northern states such as New York and New Jersey still allowed it.

Nevertheless, Jefferson's "Plan" would become the basis of the Northwest Ordinance of 1787, which laid out how

One of Congress's first orders of business was a ceremony to accept Washington's resignation of his military commission.

the Northwest Territory was to be settled and governed. In addition to prohibiting slavery, it guaranteed basic rights such as habeas corpus and trial by jury. Mainly, it let the world know that the lands south of the Great Lakes, north of the Ohio River, and east of the Mississippi would become a settled part of the United States.

In May 1784, Congress finally sent Jefferson to France. As trade minister, his task was to negotiate treaties of trade and commerce—critical to the new country's survival—with the maritime countries of Europe and North Africa. A year later, Congress would appoint him minister to the French court, replacing Benjamin Franklin, who was granted permission to retire and return home. Jefferson later recalled being frequently asked: "C'est vous, monsieur, qui remplace le Docteur Franklin?" ("It is you, sir, who replace Dr. Franklin?") He would answer: "No one can replace him, sir: I am only his successor."

When he left for France, Jefferson took Patsy with him. Polly and Lu would remain with

Jean-Antoine Houdon sculpted this famous bust of Benjamin Franklin based on observations of Franklin at public events.

his sister-in-law, Elizabeth Eppes, where they had been since their mother's death. But in January 1785, Jefferson

WHOOPING COUGH

Whooping cough, or pertussis, is a contagious disease marked by a barking cough.

received news that Lu had died from whooping cough. He immediately sent for eight-year-old Polly, so that what remained of his family could be together. She arrived late in 1787, along with a 14-year-old slave, Sally Hemings. Sally's brother James was already in France—Jefferson wanted him to learn the art of French cooking.

Jefferson understood the importance of his job in France. The United States needed revenue to pay off its debts. His goal was to obtain the right to sell American products, such as whale oil, salted meats, and tobacco, in foreign countries. It was a tall order. European nations weren't interested in forming trade agreements with the new, bankrupt republic. He did make some headway with the French, negotiating lower duties on American products. And he and John Adams managed to get a $400,000 loan from Dutch bankers.

Patsy Jefferson was her father's constant companion. During his first term as president, Patsy filled the role of first lady.

Congress also sent Jefferson and Adams to negotiate with the North African Barbary nations: Morocco, Algiers, Tripoli, and Tunis. For years, Barbary pirates had terrorized the North Atlantic, capturing the ships of any country that refused to pay a tribute to Barbary rulers. Cargo was seized, and crews held for ransom.

As part of the British Empire, colonial ships had been protected by the Royal Navy and by treaties between Britain and the Barbary nations. During the Revolutionary War, the 1778 Treaty of Alliance with France provided French protection over colonial ships. But now, Americans sailed the seas without protection.

On principle, Jefferson opposed the payment of ransoms. He tried to form an association of countries to stand up to the Barbary pirates, but the plan fell through. Even though the treasury couldn't afford it, Congress saw no choice but to pay the tribute to the tune of one million dollars per year.

Jefferson's years in Paris were among the happiest in his life. The Enlightenment as an intellectual and political movement was at its peak; he worked closely with two men he admired, Adams and Franklin; he lived in a grand residence on the Champs-Elysées called the Hôtel de Langeac, which even had a flush toilet.

For hundreds of years, Barbary pirates were a scourge of the Mediterranean. Many of their captives were sold into slavery.

One of Jefferson's favorite pastimes was to attend performances at the Théâtre Français, Paris's largest theater.

Jefferson traveled all over Europe, from Amsterdam to Strasbourg, usually in his own carriage drawn by horses. As in his early college days, he spent his leisure time at concerts and in bookshops. Almost every day, he walked through the beautiful Tuileries Gardens, facing the river Seine, where he watched the launch of hot-air balloons carrying passengers.

Jefferson immersed himself in French culture, especially its architecture, art, and music. He dressed in French clothing and wigs, and became an expert on French wines. He sketched the buildings he saw, including a Roman temple that became a model for Richmond's capitol building.

Many of his friends had asked to read *Notes on the State of Virginia,* so Jefferson ordered a 200-copy printing of it in Paris. It wasn't meant for the public, but a bookseller got his hands on a copy and published a French version without permission. Jefferson wrote: "I never had seen so wretched an attempt at translation." When a London bookseller asked to print the original, Jefferson agreed. Soon, the author of the *Notes* became highly sought after as a guest in the Paris salons.

Jefferson sat for his first known portrait in London in 1786. He purchased it for 10 pounds.

In 1786, Jefferson went to London to help John Adams, now ambassador to England, negotiate with the ambassador of Tripoli. The negotiations didn't go well, but the trip wasn't a total waste of time.

While in England, Jefferson took some time to look around. He thought English gardens the most magnificent in the world, but considered London's architecture "the most wretched style I ever saw." He visited the house where Shakespeare was born and saw the Magna Carta at the British Museum.

During this time, Jefferson and Adams met with King George III and Queen Charlotte. However, their reception was decidedly cold—the king (perhaps still upset about the revolution) turned his back to the American envoys and walked away. "It was impossible for anything to be more ungracious," Jefferson wrote.

Soon after his return to Paris, Jefferson, now 43, became smitten with a beautiful, accomplished Englishwoman, 27-year-old Maria Cosway. He was charmed by her compositions for the

MAGNA CARTA

England's Magna Carta, issued in 1215, guaranteed rights to British citizens.

harp and harpsichord. Unfortunately, she was married to a man 20 years her senior, who treated his wife with indifference. For six weeks, Jefferson spent every day with Maria. He described that time as "filled to the brim with happiness." The innocent romance ended when the Cosways returned to London.

During this time, Jefferson fractured his right wrist, an injury from which he never completely recovered. It made it difficult for him to hold a pen, let alone his beloved violin. One account alleged that he broke his wrist while jumping over a hedge to meet Maria Cosway. Jefferson would only say that it "would be a long story for the left [hand] to tell."

In America, the new government was being put to its first major test. Small farmers were being taxed unfairly, and the many who couldn't pay were sent to debtors' prisons. On September 26, 1786, Daniel Shays, a former captain in the Continental Army, led about 800 farmers in a confrontation with as many Massachusetts militiamen. When Shays' rebellion spread to other states, it seemed that civil war was possible. Shays was defeated on February 2, 1787, but the rebellion led to reforms in the Massachusetts legislature that influenced the composition of the U.S. Constitution.

Maria Cosway was a talented musician and painter, as well as a great beauty.

One of the central questions behind the drafting of the U.S. Constitution was how much power the federal government should have.

Because he was in Paris, Jefferson was absent from the 1787 Constitutional Convention in Philadelphia, where the problems of governing the new nation were debated. The Articles of Confederation were replaced with the new Constitution of the United States, which provided for a stronger central government. Jefferson received updates from James Madison, and in turn wrote to Madison about the growing turmoil in Paris.

At the time, France was still governed by privileged groups, while working classes were taxed to pay for foreign wars, court extravagances, and rising national debt. In the harsh winter of 1788–1789, hundreds died of starvation, and French citizens were growing restless.

On March 4, 1789, the U.S. Constitution went into effect. George Washington became the nation's first president. The Senate wanted to give him the title of "His Highness George Washington, President of the United States, and Protector of their Liberties." In the end, they settled for just "President."

Ten weeks later, revolution erupted in France. Jefferson worried that things would get out of hand. Yet in spite of the French Revolution's bloody course, which included the execution of many of his friends, Jefferson continued to put faith in its democratic ideals. He had worked with the Marquis de Lafayette on a charter of rights and a new French constitution. As author of the Declaration of Independence, Jefferson must have found these events fascinating to watch.

In their letters, Jefferson and Madison debated the merits of adding a bill of rights to the U.S. Constitution to spell out the rights of citizens. Madison argued against it on the grounds that those rights were already protected by the Constitution. But Jefferson managed to change his mind—in the end, Madison was the Bill of Rights's main author. After months of debate, Congress approved the final version on September 25, 1789.

On September 28, Jefferson, Patsy, Polly, and James and Sally Hemings boarded a ship to sail home. Under French law, James could have claimed freedom in France. But he returned to Virginia to train another slave to cook. Jefferson promised to free him once he had. (And he was true to his word.)

It wasn't until Jefferson landed in Virginia nearly a month later that he learned of his appointment as secretary of state. He wasn't sure he wanted the job, but President Washington insisted. At age 46, Jefferson had to postpone his dreams of a quiet life at Monticello once again.

Freedom of Religion

The Bill of Rights was influenced by Jefferson's Virginia Statute for Religious Freedom, written in 1779 and enacted into state law in 1786 after years of bitter debate. It advocates separation of church and state, and gave Jefferson the reputation of being an enemy of religion.

chapter **6**

Secretary of State

Secretary Jefferson found himself frequently disagreeing with Washington's administration. The leaders of the American Revolution had envisioned a government for the people by the people, but that was just vague enough to get them into trouble. Jefferson believed that the government was veering away from the principles of the revolution.

As secretary of state, Jefferson's primary concern was foreign affairs. And with Britain, France, and Spain in conflict, there was plenty to keep him busy. Privately he supported France, but he believed that the United States should stay out of foreign wars. This put him at odds with treasury secretary Alexander Hamilton, who was eager to make the new nation a world power. Hamilton saw Jefferson as an apologist for the bloody excesses of the French Revolution. Jefferson saw Hamilton as "bewitched . . . by the British example" of aristocratic, anti-democratic values.

President Washington tried to keep the peace between Alexander Hamilton and Thomas Jefferson.

To President Washington's disappointment, the division over foreign and domestic affairs gave rise to rival political parties. Hamilton and his allies, called Federalists, wanted more power for the federal government. The Democratic-Republicans, led by Jefferson, Madison, and others, fought for a strict interpretation of the Constitution, and stronger rights for states and individuals.

Alexander Hamilton would feud with Jefferson on both domestic and foreign affairs throughout the 1790s.

As treasury secretary, Hamilton wanted to establish a strong economic system to pay off America's debts and support a prosperous nation. Under the weak Articles of Confederation, the Continental Congress had been unable to collect taxes for defense. To pay for the war, the government had taken out foreign loans, and issued promissory notes to Americans in exchange for supplies. Now that the war was over, it was time to pay.

Hamilton proposed a Bank of the United States, the country's first central bank, and suggested that the federal government assume the war debts carried by the states.

FEDERAL

Federal issues pertain to the national or central government.

Jefferson thought this would give the central government too much power and would be downright unconstitutional. In the words of

L'Enfant's design for the capital city was beautiful, but he himself became known for being bossy and overbearing.

Thomas Paine, he believed "that government is best which governs the least." But in the end, the Democratic-Republicans supported Hamilton's plan. In exchange, the Federalists agreed to support a plan to build the nation's capital in the south. These were compromises intended to strengthen the Union, including the rich, commercial North, with its capital in the slave-owning rural South.

At a dinner party hosted by Jefferson, George Washington chose the site for the capital of the new nation. Most capitals were built on existing towns or settlements. For example,

Paris was built on the old Roman town of Lutetia. But here was a rare chance for America to take historic, social, and political considerations into account in the building of its capital. The new "Federal City" was to be built on the Potomac River, where Virginia and Maryland converged.

The area now called Washington, District of Columbia, was at that time a swampy wilderness. Disease-carrying mosquitoes lived in the marshes, which had to be drained to get rid of them. Pigs roamed wild. It would take city planners 10 years to transform the land into a worthy capital city.

President Washington appointed Pierre Charles L'Enfant to design the new capital, and three commissioners to supervise the work. It was L'Enfant who decided to set the Capitol Building on one hill and the President's House on another. Jefferson helped design the layout of the city, and approved L'Enfant's street-and-boulevard plan. But he also found himself having to mediate disagreements between L'Enfant and the commissioners. In the end, L'Enfant proved impossible to work with, and Washington dismissed him.

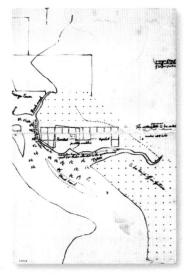

Jefferson made this sketch of the new nation's capital in 1791.

Planning was handed over to Andrew and Joseph Ellicott, who had

Jefferson and the Media

Jefferson was one of the first Americans who understood the importance of press coverage. It allowed the people to scrutinize their leaders and make sure they had nothing to hide. Jefferson made use of the *National Gazette* and the *General Advertiser*, which supported his party's positions, as opposed to the *Gazette of the United States*, which represented the Federalists' viewpoint.

conducted the survey of the city's boundaries. They largely followed L'Enfant's plans, adding many of the parks and streets that Washington, D.C., is known for today.

In 1792, Jefferson announced a contest to design the President's House. Washington chose the winner, an Irish immigrant named James Hoban, and added some ideas of his own—including enlarging Hoban's design by 30 percent.

Meanwhile, the conflict between Jefferson and Hamilton was getting nastier. They began to attack each other in the press, and those attacks escalated until President Washington urged them to stop. Jefferson wanted to resign at that point, but decided that would make it look as though he were running away from the bad press.

Jefferson continued to serve as secretary of state, and monitor developments in Europe. In France, the revolution was growing bloodier. King Louis XVI had been sent to the guillotine, initiating a period known as the Reign of Terror. The monarchy was abolished, and France was declared

GUILLOTINE

A guillotine is a device that beheads prisoners by dropping a heavy blade from above.

Edmond-Charles Genêt jeopardized American neutrality by capturing British ships and their crews.

a republic. First the French nobility and then regular citizens had their heads chopped off. Jefferson's friend Lafayette was arrested for treason and held prisoner for five years.

Other European countries were alarmed by events in France and declared war on the new republic. Britain was in almost continual conflict with France until the end of the Napoleonic Wars in 1815. Jefferson supported the French, and Alexander Hamilton supported the British.

In April 1793, the new Republic of France sent a minister, Edmond-Charles Genêt, to America to gain support for France's wars with Spain and Britain. He asked the United States to give up its neutrality. Jefferson refused.

Genêt defied Jefferson by recruiting American crews and preparing them for attacks on British ships and Spanish lands in Louisiana and Florida. But when his political party fell in France, he backed off. If Genêt had gone home at this point, he would have been sent to the guillotine—so Washington granted him asylum, and he lived on happily in New York. At the

ASYLUM

Asylum is government protection granted to foreign citizens who face political persecution in their own countries.

end of that year, Jefferson resigned as secretary of state at the sprightly age of 50.

The new secretary of state, Edmund Randolph, asked Jefferson to negotiate a new treaty with Spain, but that was the last thing he wanted to do. "I am going to Virginia," he wrote. "I am then to be liberated from the hated occupations of politics, and to remain in the bosom of my family, my farm, and my books."

Jefferson spent the next three years building and improving Monticello. His head was filled with ideas for modernizing the estate. The wooden plows of the day hardly scratched the surface. Jefferson developed a "moldboard" plow to improve soil drainage. He also imported a mechanical thresher from Scotland that reduced the need for slave labor.

Tending to his farm wasn't just something Jefferson loved to do; it needed to be done. In his 10-year absence, Monticello had been left in the hands of neglectful overseers and was in sore need of attention. Plus, Jefferson was in debt, partly inherited from his mother's and father-in-law's estates, made worse by natural disasters that had affected his farms, and the state of the national economy. Jefferson didn't earn much in public service, and he often had to pay for things out of his own pocket. His land needed to be more productive. So Jefferson experimented with crop rotation, the use of fertilizer, and different species of plants. When he lived in Paris, Jefferson sent seeds back home, and he introduced many vegetables to America that are now commonplace, such as eggplant, brussels sprouts, cauliflower, and broccoli. He grew grapes to make wine, and tried brewing different beers. Most of the crops fed the people and animals that lived at Monticello, but he also grew wheat to sell for profit. When all that wasn't enough, he borrowed money to build a nail factory, which supplied all the stores in the area. But even with all his ingenuity, Jefferson never paid off all his debts.

Monticello was full of Jefferson's mechanical gadgets, which he installed for personal comfort. In a recess at the foot of his bed was an unusual "clothes horse." This organizer had 48 projecting limbs on which clothes were hung. In 1804 he installed double doors that were made to open simultaneously by a mechanism hidden in the floor.

During his brief retirement, Jefferson welcomed many visitors to the house, including his grandchildren, who were often seen playing on the lawn. His grandson, Thomas Jefferson Randolph, later recalled that his grandfather would play the violin while the children danced around him.

Jefferson doted on his grandchildren. His daughter Patsy had 12 children. Polly had three, though only one lived to adulthood.

chapter **7**

Enemies Abroad and at Home

Jefferson wasn't completely isolated from government matters at Monticello. He knew that Hamilton and his group were up to their old antics, and he wasn't happy about it. "From the moment of my retiring from the administration," he later wrote, "the Federalists got unchecked hold on General Washington."

Federal tax collectors were attacked by angry citizens during the Whiskey Rebellion. One officer was covered with tar and feathers.

In 1794, a revolt known as the Whiskey Rebellion broke out

in western Pennsylvania in protest of Hamilton's federal tax on distilling liquor. Ultimately, Washington himself led a group of soldiers from several states to suppress the rebels. Jefferson didn't like the tax, but he liked the excessive show of military force even less. The force of 12,950 men was roughly the size of the entire Continental Army.

Jefferson also objected to the Jay Treaty—negotiated by John Jay, Washington's envoy to London—which formed closer ties between the United States and Britain. Jefferson didn't trust the British. They were still occupying numerous western posts within the United States, seizing American ships and cargo, and forcing American sailors into the service of the Royal Navy—a practice known as impressment that had been going on since the mid-17th century. Many Americans didn't like the Jay Treaty because it ignored these issues, and the French didn't like it because it was an alliance with one of the countries with whom they were at war.

Once again, Jefferson and Hamilton fell on two sides of the fence, with Jefferson calling the treaty a "monument of folly," and Hamilton giving it his support.

Jefferson was happy to hear that Washington, who tended to side with Hamilton, would be retiring. He was less happy about being picked by his party as a top candidate in the 1796 presidential election. This would be the first election where political parties each campaigned for, or supported, a candidate. The same old accusations were flung from both sides. Posters and pamphlets accused

Jefferson of sympathizing with France's Reign of Terror, and of being an atheist.

According to the Constitution, the candidate who came in second in the election became vice president, regardless of what party he belonged to (and whether he had anything in common with the president). As a result, John Adams, a Federalist, became president, and Jefferson, a Democratic-Republican, became vice president—which meant they were in for a bumpy ride. The framers of the Constitution never saw this coming, because when it was written, there were no political parties.

Before leaving office, Adams appointed many of Jefferson's Federalist enemies to government posts. The "midnight appointments" ended their friendship.

Soon Jefferson's old arguments with Hamilton were repeating themselves, only this time with President Adams. These disputes began to dissolve the friendship between Jefferson and Adams. With Britain and France still at war, President Adams asked Congress to allocate a large sum of money to enlarge the navy and raise an army. France was attacking American ships, claiming that they contained British supplies, and Adams felt that an expanded miltary was necessary to defend American interests.

For Jefferson, there were two problems with Adams's plan: the expansion of federal power, and the possibility that America would go to war with France. Jefferson didn't want either. He believed that the French didn't really want to go to war. They were just annoyed with the Jay Treaty and America's refusal to pay its debts. (The United States claimed that its debt to the government of Louis XVI had ended when Louis was executed.)

The Federalists, who favored Britain, spread rumors that the French were sending spies to the United States and planning future attacks, thus escalating tensions. In May 1798, Adams authorized the newly fortified U.S. Navy to attack French ships. In July, Congress canceled its treaties with France, and began the fighting in earnest. This war at sea was called the Quasi-War, because neither side had actually declared war.

That summer, Congress also passed four laws that were supposed to protect the United States from "dangerous" foreigners—but in fact they were used by the Federalists to silence their opponents. It was just the kind of expansion of governmental power that Jefferson feared, and he referred to the hysteria as the "reign of witches."

Jefferson found many parts of the Alien and Sedition Acts objectionable. One of the

> *"A little patience, and we shall see this reign of witches pass."*
>
> –Thomas Jefferson

laws made it a crime to publish "any false, scandalous and malicious writing." This seemed to violate the rights of free speech and a free press, as protected by the Constitution. The law resulted in the arrest of 25 newspaper editors, most of whom were Democratic-Republicans.

Jefferson called the hugely unpopular Acts "an experiment on the American mind to see how far it will bear an avowed violation of the Constitution." Even today, when new laws are introduced, there is often a question of how much power the federal government should be given and how much should remain in the hands of the state or the individual.

Napoleon was on his way to conquering all of Europe, having defeated two coalitions of European nations. After 1800, only Britain was left to fight him.

Meanwhile, in France, there was a new chief in town. The great military leader Napoleon Bonaparte came to power in November 1799, declaring that the French Revolution was over. It was already becoming clear to President Adams that America's involvement in the Quasi-War was costly and pointless.

Since the new French leader was willing to negotiate, Adams sent a peace delegation to Paris in April 1800.

Napoleon had built his reputation by conquering lands as far as Egypt, eventually rising to become First Consul of France. (Later, he made himself Emperor.) After the French and Indian War, France had lost its lands east of the Mississippi, as well as Canada, to Britain, and the lands west of the Mississippi, including New Orleans, to Spain. Napoleon wanted them back. He hoped to restore France's empire in North America.

At the time, Louisiana consisted of the entire Mississippi valley, from the Appalachians to the Rockies. In 1800, Napoleon signed a secret treaty with Spain returning control of Louisiana to the French. As neighbors, the Spanish had been cooperative, even giving Americans the right to use the ports in New Orleans, which was increasing in importance as the economy in the west developed. The power-hungry Napoleon was certain to be less accommodating. In any case, the actual transfer of power didn't take place for three years, during which time France's resources were taken up by conflict in the West Indies and continuing wars in Europe.

Meanwhile, in 1800, the United States held its fourth presidential election. When the votes were counted, there was a tie between two candidates from the same party: Thomas Jefferson and Aaron Burr, a New York senator. The Federalist candidates, John Adams and Thomas Pinckney of South Carolina, received fewer votes than either of their Democratic-Republican opponents.

Amending the Constitution

The Constitution was written to stand the test of time—but the founders knew that they couldn't possibly cover every eventuality. The fifth article, or section, of the Constitution allows for amendments to be proposed and approved by Congress. Amendments generally serve either to correct problems in the main document (as in the case of electoral rules) or to adapt to changing times (as in allowing all people to vote, regardless of race or gender). The first 10 amendments to the Constitution are known as the Bill of Rights.

Just like the 1796 election—in which candidates from rival parties were elected to the two highest offices—this election exposed flaws in the Constitution. Four years later, an amendment would be adopted to fix the problem. Under the Twelfth Amendment, Jefferson and Burr would have been running mates, with one clearly running as his party's presidential candidate and the other running as the vice-presidential candidate. At present, however, although they were in the same party, the presidential contest came down to Jefferson and Burr.

The vote was thrown to the Federalist-controlled House of Representatives, which had to decide which of the men was the lesser of two evils. The House was deadlocked, but its members agreed that they would vote continually until a president was chosen. The battle for votes took so long that many worried there wouldn't be a president to take office when Adams's term ended.

Meanwhile, a rumor went around of a Federalist conspiracy to assassinate Jefferson.

To anyone who read the newspapers, neither candidate may have seemed appealing. The entire election had been one of the most corrosive in American history, full of accusations and slander. One particularly potent example of the mudslinging that took place appeared in the *Connecticut Courant*, a Hartford newspaper, which warned that if Jefferson was elected, "murder, robbery, rape, adultery and incest will openly be taught and practiced." Jefferson was an ardent supporter of freedom of the press, but such articles must have put his beliefs to the test.

In the meantime, the Democrat-Republicans printed stories claiming that candidate John Adams was a fool and a criminal.

Jefferson was called a madman and an atheist. The latter part of this rumor at least had some basis in truth. Although Jefferson was not an atheist, he believed that an official state church, such as the one in England, was contrary to the freedom of religion guaranteed in the Bill of Rights.

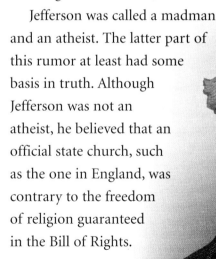

Jefferson lost to Adams in the 1796 presidential election, making him vice president. He made sure to hone his campaign skills for the next election.

Dueling

Alexander Hamilton died in 1804 after a pistol duel with Aaron Burr. In those days, dueling was a popular way to deal with personal conflicts. According to custom, apologies could be offered until combat began, and the duel called off. The chance of dying in a pistol duel was pretty small, because accuracy was difficult and the guns often misfired.

A Baltimore newspaper even broke the story that Jefferson was dead, only to be contradicted by another headline that proclaimed him to be alive. Jefferson ignored it all and actively campaigned for the presidency. He saw things differently now than he had in 1796, when he wrote to Adams, "I have no ambition to govern men." In his view, the current state of the government threatened not only the Constitution but also the survival of the nation itself. He wasn't going to sit back and watch it happen.

In spite of his contentious relationship with Jefferson, Alexander Hamilton was instrumental in getting Jefferson elected. In September, Hamilton had written a 50-page pamphlet that was extremely critical of Adams. It backfired and was damaging both to the Federalist Party and to Hamilton's own political career. He became determined that Adams should not win reelection, and placed his support behind fellow Federalist Thomas Pinckney.

Ultimately, Pinckney came in fourth. After the election, when the House was deciding between Jefferson and Burr, Hamilton wrote to other Federalists: "Jefferson is to be preferred. He is by far not so dangerous a man and he has pretentions to character." Hamilton not only found Burr to be devoid of moral principles—he also feared that Burr, a notorious opportunist, might change parties and challenge his leadership of the Federalists.

Hamilton worked to persuade his Federalist colleagues to switch votes from Burr to Jefferson. While ballots were cast over and over in the House, Hamilton wrote to John Bayard of Delaware that Burr was "the most unfit man in the United States for the office of President." In the end, Bayard tipped the scales by abstaining, and Jefferson was elected President of the United States. Burr became his vice president. In spite of these election battles, the government changed hands without bloodshed, proving that, basically, the Constitution was doing its job.

Aaron Burr won praise for his fairness as president of the Senate. But after the bitter campaign, Jefferson shut him out of party matters.

chapter **8**

Mr. President

"The President's House is in a beautiful situation in front of which is the Potomac with a view of Alexandria," wrote Abigail Adams to her sister. "The country around is romantic but wild, a wilderness at present."

Jefferson was the first president to live in the mansion now known as the White House for a full term. Before moving in, he added two coal-burning fireplaces and two bathrooms. With the help of architect Benjamin Latrobe, he designed two long colonnades on the east and west sides of the house.

The site of the new federal city consisted largely of rolling hills, farmland, and wetlands along the Potomac River.

The White House was decorated with the comfort of its residents in mind. Jefferson filled his office there with maps, globes, charts, and books. He kept a pet mockingbird, which frequent visitor Margaret Bayard Smith wrote was "the constant companion of his solitary and studious hours." Jefferson would release it from its cage to fly around the room. It would rest on a table and sing, or sit on his shoulders to take food from his mouth. "How he loved this bird!" wrote Smith.

While he lived in the mansion, Jefferson made many improvements,

Dolley Madison

Usually, the president's wife hosted parties at the White House. Since Jefferson was a widower, it was often up to Dolley Madison, the wife of secretary of state James Madison, to assume that role. Dolley was a natural hostess who continued in her role at the White House when her husband became president for two terms.

including a built-in dumbwaiter that allowed meals to be served and dishes to be taken away without the interruption of servants. He also made a careful plan for the gardens, so that every season had its bloom. In the greenhouse, he grew flowers, both common and exotic, and fragrant plants such as orange trees.

President Jefferson also gave dinner parties, welcoming politicians, foreign diplomats, and local gentry. This painting depicts the Capitol building as it appeared in 1800, when the U.S. Congress first occupied it.

In addition to fine wines, he delighted in serving European treats such as peach flambé, macaroni, and macaroons. However, he abandoned French fashions for more casual dress. His guests often found him wearing slippers.

On March 4, 1801, 57-year-old Jefferson was sworn in as president. The inaugural ceremony was designed to show that he was one of the people, and had their interests at heart. He even walked—

INAUGURAL

An inaugural event is the first; specifically, one occurring upon formal entry into a position or office.

instead of riding in a carriage—from his boarding house to the Capitol, a short distance away.

The nation's capital had moved from Philadelphia to Washington, D.C., only a few months before. Jefferson was the first president to take an oath of office at the unfinished Capitol building. John Adams was conspicuously absent, disappointed that he hadn't been reelected.

Jefferson made it clear in his speech that he wanted to restore the ideals of the American Revolution, and urged people to value its principles and secure them for future generations. His envisioned "a wise and frugal Government, which shall restrain men from injuring one another, shall leave them otherwise free to regulate their own pursuits of industry and improvement, and shall not take from the mouth of labor the bread it had earned."

He also outlined the goals for his presidency, which included "economy in the public expense" and "the honest payment of our debts." (Within three years, his government would reduce taxes and pay off the national debt.) In foreign affairs, he called for "peace, commerce, and honest friendship with all nations . . . " In other words, he felt the government

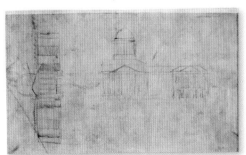

Jefferson submitted this plan anonymously to a contest for the design of the Capitol building, but it was not chosen.

should ignore aggression and not get in the way of commercial interests.

Finally, Jefferson reached out to his political opponents in his speech. He wanted to heal the rift between the two parties. It was in his interest to gain the support of the Federalist-controlled Congress. Nevertheless, he remained suspicious of the Federalists, and removed many of them from his administration. Instead, he appointed competent, loyal friends to advise him.

As for Aaron Burr, Jefferson never trusted his vice president. On the other hand, Burr's power was limited. John Adams once described the vice presidency as "the most insignificant office that ever the invention of man contrived or his imagination conceived."

One of the immediate changes that took place when Jefferson became president was that tributes to the Barbary pirates would no longer

Captain Bainbridge saw action in the First and Second Barbary Wars. No other U.S. naval captain lost as many ships, but he had also won impressive victories.

be paid. The Pasha of Tripoli demanded that America pay him $225,000 immediately and $25,000 every year thereafter. Jefferson refused. On May 10, 1801, Tripoli declared war on the United States. Its allies, Morocco, Algiers, and Tunis, soon joined in.

Although Jefferson had always sought reduced spending and a small navy, he didn't hesitate to make good use of the navy and marine corps that had been built up during John Adams's presidency. He sent four American warships to blockade Tripoli's ports. It was a difficult job to control a coastline 1,200 miles (1931 km) long, but the show of force gradually convinced Morocco, Tunis, and Algeria to break their alliance with Tripoli.

An embarrassing setback occurred when the frigate *Philadelphia* ran aground off the African coast. Captain William Bainbridge had the cannons thrown overboard and the foremast cut away in hopes that lightening the load would free the ship. Finally, Captain Bainbridge had no choice but to surrender his ship and crew of 300 sailors to the Pasha of Tripoli. The captured Americans were held as slaves, and the enemy now had America's fastest, best-equipped warship in its possession. The story made headlines around the world.

Commodore Edward Preble, a veteran of the Continental Navy, decided that the *Philadelphia* could not be rescued and had to be destroyed. So he sent

FRIGATE

A frigate is a medium-sized warship.

a raiding party led by Lieutenant Stephen Decatur to burn the frigate. The party traveled on a captured Tripolitan ship to avoid detection, but the ruse was quickly discovered. After a hand-to-hand skirmish, the Americans burned the *Philadelphia* and made their escape. Lieutenant Decatur became a national hero.

The USS *Philadelphia* was burned in Tripoli Harbor rather than being left in the hands of the enemy.

The First Barbary War lasted for four years, extending into Jefferson's second term as president. During this time, Commodore Preble launched a series of battles, but they didn't have much effect. In 1805, Jefferson reluctantly agreed to a plan proposed by William Eaton, the former American consul of Tunis, to capture the Pasha of Tripoli and replace him with his brother, Hamet, who was exiled in Egypt and had agreed to cooperate with the Americans. Eaton departed with very little support from Jefferson, who didn't want to be connected with the scheme if it failed. Eaton complained, "I am ordered on the expedition . . . without any special instructions to regulate my conduct; without even a letter to the ally to whom I am directed."

MERCENARIES

Mercenaries are soldiers hired to fight for a foreign country.

Eaton brought together an army of Greek, Arab, and Berber mercenaries, reinforced by a detachment of U.S. marines. They marched across the desert with a caravan of camels from Alexandria, Egypt, and arrived at the Tripolitan port of Derna. Three American ships waited there to provide offshore bombardment. Two days later, Eaton launched an attack in alliance with Hamet, and captured the town of Derna. It was the first recorded land engagement of American troops on foreign soil.

Eaton didn't know that while he was making plans to take the battle to Tripoli's capital city, the Pasha had made overtures of peace. A treaty was signed in 1805 that required the United States to pay a ransom of $60,000 for Captain Bainbridge and the crew of the *Philadelphia*, but required no further tribute. Finally, Jefferson was able to report in his sixth annual message to Congress on December 2, 1806: "The states on the coast of Barbary seem generally disposed at present to respect our peace and friendship."

In fact, the Barbary pirates resumed their attacks on American vessels the following year, taking advantage of America's preoccupation with a crisis that culminated in the War of 1812. The United States returned to paying ransom for hostages, and in 1815 went to war with Algiers. After several naval victories, the Americans secured a treaty ending the payment of tribute by the United States once and for all.

chapter 9

The Louisiana Purchase

President Jefferson's next foreign-policy crisis originated closer to home, on the island of Hispaniola in the French West Indies. The fighting that began there was essentially an extension of the French Revolution in the New World. However, this revolution was carried out by slaves against their masters. At the time, no one could foresee that this conflict would lead to one of the most important developments in the history of the United States: the Louisiana Purchase.

Part of Hispaniola, Santo Domingo, belonged to Spain. The other part, Saint-Domingue (now called Haiti), belonged to France. Saint-Domingue was rich and prosperous, thanks to its sugar-cane plantations. It was also a key port for traffic between America and Europe.

For years, tension had been growing between slave-owning whites, who wanted independence from

Born a slave, Toussaint L'Ouverture went on to lead his country to freedom.

France, and whites who opposed slavery. In August 1791, the slaves themselves openly revolted. Thousands of people were killed and plantations and cities were destroyed. Similar rebellions later erupted elsewhere in the West Indies.

In Saint-Domingue, a brilliant military leader arose. Toussaint L'Ouverture was a slave who enlisted with the French forces on the island. He trained four thousand black troops in guerrilla warfare and directed them to take back Saint-Domingue for the French. But once he controlled the colony, he decided it would be better to create an independent state. To do so, he would have to fight the British and the Spanish, who both had claims to the island, as well as Napoleon's forces.

When Jefferson took office, the Haitian Revolution had already been in swing for nine years. President Adams and his administration had supported L'Ouverture, sending supplies and American ships. Jefferson was appalled. He was a known supporter of revolutions, even when they went out of control as the French Revolution had. But when it came to a slave rebellion, he had the outlook of a Southern landowner. He feared that an "expulsion of whites" in Saint-Domingue would inspire rebellion in the southern slave states. "Unless something is done, and soon done," he wrote, "we shall be the murderers of our own children . . . the revolutionary storm, now sweeping the globe, will be upon us."

GUERRILLA

Guerrilla warfare is conducted by unofficial groups, usually through sabotage and harassment.

Yellow Fever

Yellow Fever gets its name from the jaundice (yellowish appearance) experienced by many of its sufferers. It is a contagious and deadly disease, mainly transmitted by mosquitoes, that wiped out more than half the French army during the Haitian Revolution. Sufferers may bleed internally, so they often vomit blood. A vaccine was developed in the 20th century.

Jefferson deplored the slave revolt in Haiti, but without it, the United States might look very different today. Napoleon really had his sights on New Orleans, and the American West beyond it. In 1800, a secret treaty with Spain had, on paper at least, ceded Louisiana back to France. However, the French had not yet been able to return to take control of the coveted territory. In the meantime, the Spanish remained in New Orleans, while French resources were tied up with the rebellion in Saint-Domingue. Napoleon sent a fleet to Haiti under the command of General Charles Leclerc. Unfortunately, the troops were struck by malaria and yellow fever. In one month, 3,000 French soldiers died from illness. Through the haze of their sickness, many believed that they were victims of the locally practiced Voodoo—a mystical religion that combined African, West Indian, and some Catholic traditions, and whose priests were said to cast spells and raise zombies from the dead.

In October 1802, the Spanish magistrate in New Orleans closed the port to American shipping—never mind that the Spanish ambassador in Washington insisted that his government hadn't authorized it. Many Americans, the Federalists in particular, believed the French government was behind the closure. However, it may have been bad conduct on the part of the Americans that provoked it: Smuggling and piracy were common practice in New Orleans.

At the time, transportation over land was extremely difficult. Horse-drawn wagons crept along unpaved roads marred by stones and furrows. The first transcontinental railroad wouldn't be built for another 60 years. With the port closed, agricultural goods rotted away for months on ships and in warehouses. The Federalists demanded action— namely a declaration of war on France.

Jefferson resisted the pressure to declare war. Instead, he renewed efforts to secure rights to New Orleans by peaceful means, and raised the U.S. government's offer to buy the land from France. He sent an envoy, James Monroe, to France with authorization to spend 10 million dollars to secure the rights to New Orleans and west Florida.

Jefferson worried that the purchase of foreign lands by the federal government to was "a thing beyond the Constitution." The Constitution gave Congress the power to form new states, but the Louisiana Territory was French, and its inhabitants were foreign subjects. Would the purchase of Louisiana amount to an occupation? Would the collection of customs or taxes by the U.S. government amount to taxation without representation?

As committed as he was to limited government, Jefferson couldn't allow France to move into the neighborhood. So he

"What will you give for the whole?"

–French foreign minister Charles Talleyrand

decided to go through with the purchase. He began drafting two Constitutional amendments to satisfy the question of propriety once and for all. "Let us go on then perfecting it," he wrote to Senator Wilson Nicholas of Virginia, "by adding, by way of amendment to the Constitution, those powers which time and trial show are still wanting." Jefferson never submitted the amendments to Congress.

With France facing certain defeat in Haiti, Napoleon needed all of his remaining resources to finance the war in Europe. By this point, France was deeply embroiled in the Napoleonic Wars, a continuation of post-revolutionary conflicts fought against various European countries. It could not afford to occupy Louisiana—and why would it? Such an action would probably only lead to another war, against an American-British alliance. Furthermore, since Christopher Columbus, explorers of of the North American interior had discovered legends of cities

In 1803, the people of New Orleans saw the French flag raised and then lowered for the last time—and the flag of the United States raised to replace it.

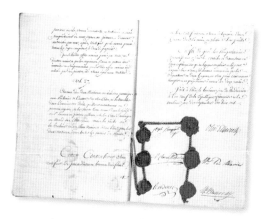

The Treaty of Louisiana ended the threat of war with France and nearly doubled the land area of the United States.

filled with treasure—but no actual gold.

Robert Livingston had been working on the purchase of New Orleans for some time without success. Now, to his surprise, Talleyrand wanted to know what the United States would pay for the entire Louisiana Territory.

Jefferson had satisfied himself that the Constitution authorized the president to make treaties, and that the purchase would fall under the scope of a treaty. Livingston and Monroe quickly agreed to a price of 15 million dollars—or about three cents an acre—for an area that would nearly double the size of the United States.

"I renounce it with the greatest regret," Napoleon told his treasury secretary, François Barbé-Marbois. "To attempt obstinately to retain it would be folly." In the end, the French flag flew over New Orleans for just a few weeks before it was replaced with the American flag. The city was transferred from Spain to France on November 30, 1803, then from France to the United States on December 20.

"Let the Land rejoice, for you have brought Louisiana for a Song," wrote General Horatio Gates to Jefferson.

The United States in 1803

Since the end of the American Revolution, thousands of American pioneers had braved

This 1803 map shows the Louisiana Territory, which encompasses all or part of 15 modern-day states and 2 Canadian provinces.

the inhospitable trails westward, hoping to stake their claims on land. Frontiersmen returned east with tales of herds of buffalo sweeping over wide prairies. East of the Mississippi, unclaimed land was becoming scarce. People there were either already property owners or unlikely ever to own land. The Louisiana Purchase would give many Americans the chance to become landowners for the very first time.

Of course, most of the west was already occupied by American Indians, who were not consulted on how their lands should be divided or governed. Eventually they would

SECEDE

To secede is to withdraw from a nation.

fight to the death to protect their land from white settlement. From time to time, they would make alliances with America's enemies.

Numerous other dilemmas came along with the new land: The boundaries of the purchased territory were unspecified, leading to continuing disputes—over Florida, in particular. And many Louisiana residents only spoke French, which made it challenging for them to learn American laws.

Jefferson was urged by Thomas Paine and James Hillhouse, a congressman from Connecticut, to keep the practice of slavery out of the newly acquired territories. They weren't asking for anything that Jefferson hadn't already proposed in the Northwest Ordinance of 1787.

However, abolishing slavery was not in the interest of plantation owners. Like tobacco, sugar farming required large numbers of slaves. Sugar was sold to make molasses, rum, and fuel. With the unrest in the West Indies, the American west became a profitable new center for sugar-cane plantations. People there were outspoken about wanting to continue the practice of slavery. Many of them wanted to secede from the United States on the basis of this issue.

In March 1807, Jefferson introduced a law to Congress prohibiting the importation of slaves. Congress passed the law. Although there were loopholes—there was no provision for stopping ships that illegally transported slaves, for instance—Jefferson could be proud of this milestone.

chapter **10**

The Second Term

In four years, President Jefferson had doubled the size of the country, repulsed the Barbary pirates, slashed army and navy spending, eliminated federal taxes, and reduced the national debt by a third. Not surprisingly, he won a second term in a landslide victory in 1804. In accordance with the newly adopted Twelfth Amendment, candidates for president and vice president ran separate races. George Clinton of New York was elected vice president.

As in his first campaign, Jefferson faced attacks in the press. The most famous of these accused him of fathering children with a slave, Sally Hemings. Sally (who had accompanied Polly to France) is believed to have been

a half-sister of Jefferson's deceased wife, and may have born a strong resemblance to her. In 1998, DNA testing indicated

Jefferson's enemies tried to ruin his reputation. In this newspaper satire, he is portrayed as a rooster courting a hen, which is supposed to represent Sally Hemings.

that Jefferson was the probable father of at least one of Hemings' children, but did not rule out other male Jeffersons, including Thomas's brother Randolph.

Jefferson never responded to the charges in public. Instead, he was preoccupied with the western expedition that was about to become a reality. Jefferson had tried three times before to organize such an expedition, but failed. His father and his teacher Reverend Maury had taught him that whoever controlled the Mississippi River could access vast western lands. At the time, no one knew what the lands held —but the Louisiana Purchase had secured access to them.

In his thirties, Jefferson's interest had been sparked again, this time by Jonathan Carver's account of his travels west. Carver was a surveyor who had attempted to find a water route to the Pacific Ocean. He had traveled an amazing distance, made some intriguing observations, and was the first English-speaking explorer to see the Rocky Mountains. In Paris, Jefferson had met John Ledyard, who further spiked his curiosity. Ledyard had sailed with the famous Captain James Cook up the Pacific coast to the Bering Strait.

In February 1803, Jefferson's expedition, called the Corps of Discovery, prepared to depart. Explorers would travel up the Missouri River to the Rocky Mountains, and then head to the Pacific Ocean—a journey of more than three years. Jefferson had chosen a reliable, intelligent, and fearless individual to lead the expedition: his personal secretary,

Dr. Rush's Bilious Pills

Dr. Benjamin Rush, a signer of the Declaration of Independence, prepared Lewis and Clark for their trip by teaching them about frontier illnesses. He also gave them a huge supply of laxatives known as "Dr. Rush's Bilious Pills"—or "Thunderclappers" as the corps called them. Traces of the pills, which contained more than 50 percent mercury, allowed future archeologists to trace the route of the expedition.

Meriweather Lewis. Lewis chose his friend William Clark to assist him.

Though he was a rugged outdoorsman, Lewis didn't have the scientific training to carry out the tasks Jefferson had outlined: collecting plant and animal specimens, mapping the river, taking note of minerals, and identifying lands that would support farming. Lewis was also to look for mastodons and mammoths—a mastodon skeleton had been excavated in New York in 1801, and some thought the extinct mammals might still be living on the continent.

So Jefferson sent Lewis to Philadelphia to be tutored in astronomy, natural history, medicine, celestial navigation, and botany. Andrew Ellicott, the surveyor who had taken part in planning Washington, D.C., taught Lewis to use a sextant and octant to calculate distance and position, and a chronometer to accurately measure time.

In the spring of 1804, Lewis, Clark, and more than 40 others (including hunters, soldiers, blacksmiths, and cooks) set out. Jefferson wanted the Corps to encourage peace and trade among the Indian tribes they encountered, and to study their cultures as thoroughly as possible. Lewis and Clark presented "peace

Lewis and Clark offered a peace medal, shown here with a peace pipe, to Indian Chiefs they met. The opposite side of the medal depicts an image of Jefferson.

medals," depicting Jefferson on one side and clasped hands on the other, to the tribes as gifts. The first tribe they met, the Yankton Sioux, were disappointed with these gifts, but the second tribe, the Teton Sioux, were positively disgusted with them. They demanded a boat instead, and it seemed as though there would be a fight. But finally Lewis and Clark were allowed to continue upriver.

It was a grueling journey. The men were chased by bears,

plagued by mosquitoes and ticks, and bitten by snakes. They fell off river bluffs, suffered frostbite,

Lewis and Clark's expedition was rough-and-tumble affair. They are shown here losing notes and specimens on the upper Missouri river.

Indians used vast expanses of water and land for their hunting and fishing lifestyles, which the U.S. government deemed inefficient.

and became ill. When they hit the Rocky Mountains, they finally realized there was no direct water route from the Mississippi to the Pacific Ocean.

From time to time, Lewis and Clark sent plant, animal, and mineral specimens back to Jefferson. Once Jefferson opened a box to find a live prairie dog sent by the explorers.

As they traveled west, Lewis and Clark met some friendly Indian tribes, and some hostile ones. America's relationship with American Indians was getting increasingly tense. After the Revolutionary War, America didn't have the financial or military strength to enter into a war for land with Indian tribes. So Congress adopted the more peaceful approach of buying land from the Indians, instead of just taking it. The lawmakers assumed that the Indians would move farther and farther west to make room for white settlers.

President Jefferson believed that American Indians could remain on their native lands, as long as they were "civilized"—that is, taught to read, write, and farm. In 1809

MISSIONARY

Missionaries are people sent to a foreign country to convert locals to a religion.

he wrote to John Jay: "The plan of civilizing the Indians is undoubtedly a great improvement on the ancient & totally ineffectual one of beginning with religious missionaries."

Traditionally, Indians made use of great expanses of land for hunting and fishing. But Jefferson believed that they could be taught to live with less land, making room for white settlers. He was a man of his time when he described this as "a coincidence of interests." Eventually, he came to believe that assimilation to white culture was critical to the Indians' survival.

Jefferson met with various Indian delegations to encourage them to stop hunting and take up the plow instead. He told the Miami and Potawatomi Indians: "We shall, with great pleasure, see your people become disposed to cultivate the earth, to raise herds of useful animals and to spin and weave, for their food and clothing. These resources are certain, they will never disappoint you, while those of hunting may fail, and expose your women and children to the miseries of hunger and cold."

He promised that Indians would retain control of their traditional lands unless they chose to sell. The government would provide them with plows, livestock, and instructions on cultivating soil.

However, Jefferson underestimated the reluctance of Indians to give up their lands and way of life. And it was becoming clear to the Indians that the Americans weren't playing fair:

Indian Languages

Jefferson had Lewis and Clark take detailed notes on the Indian languages they came across. This was a keen interest throughout his life. He had already tried to catalog the different tribes in *Notes on Virginia,* and he studied the subject extensively during his presidency. In his first year as president, he held a reception for five Cherokee chiefs, during which he questioned them about their vocabulary.

A system of trading posts put Indians in debt, which they could only settle by selling their lands. And whenever fighting occurred, Americans seized Indian lands as the price for peace.

Jefferson also failed to anticipate resistance from white pioneers, who didn't want Indian farmers for neighbors. Instead, the pioneers had a habit of simply claiming Indian lands as their own—and the U.S. army was unable to stop them. By the time of Lewis and Clark's expedition, the American Indian population had dropped dramatically. The Indians were being been wiped out by wars between tribes and their European allies, as well as diseases.

By November 1805, Lewis and Clark had reached the Pacific Ocean. They camped for the winter, spending the time collecting specimens and recording their observations, and then headed back east at last.

Meanwhile, Jefferson was struggling with foreign policy as well. The British and French were still caught up in the Napoleonic Wars, battling for world supremacy, and America was caught in the middle. The two naval powers, each believing that the United States was supplying the other with arms and supplies, regularly attacked American ships. With sailors in short supply, the British turned to their old habit of impressment. They often stopped American vessels in search of deserters claiming to be American citizens. Even some who actually were citizens were nonetheless forced into service.

The United States was further infuriated when British warships stationed themselves just outside U.S. harbors, boarding and searching American ships within American waters. This state of affairs made it increasingly difficult for the United States to remain neutral, and gave Jefferson another bout of his crippling headaches.

In June 1807, America came close to declaring war on Britain when the British warship *Leopard* stopped the American frigate *Chesapeake* off the coast of Norfolk, Virginia. In a small boat, a British lieutenant approached the frigate demanding that the *Chesapeake* submit to a search for supposed deserters. Captain James Barron refused, and the lieutenant rowed back to his ship.

The *Leopard*'s gunports opened and its guns prepared to fire. The crew of the *Chesapeake* scrambled for defenses. The *Leopard* opened fire for 15 minutes, killing 3 men and wounding 18 others. The *Chesapeake* was thoroughly unprepared—its powder flasks were stored away in the hold—and only managed to fire a single gun before surrendering. The ship was boarded, and four crewmembers were arrested for desertion.

In fact, only one of them was British. Two of them were African-Americans. Nevertheless, all four were put on trial. The British citizen was sentenced to death and hanged. The three Americans were sentenced to a whipping, but the sentence was later commuted.

Americans were shocked that the *Chesapeake* had put up so little resistance and surrendered so quickly. Jefferson resisted pressure to declare war on Britain over this incident. He felt that he could bring Britain to terms by applying economic pressure instead. Unfortunately, this resulted in the ill-conceived Embargo Act of 1807.

Under this act, international trade to and from American ports was forbidden. Jefferson wanted to teach England and France that they couldn't survive without American trade. However, it was the U.S. economy that suffered most. Shipbuilders,

The USS *Chesapeake* was later captured during the War of 1812. In this painting, a British ship tows the unlucky American vessel into Halifax Harbor in Canada.

manufacturers, and merchants from the commercial north were hurt, and southern farmers suffered massive losses.

The revenue of the federal government, derived almost entirely from customs duties, dropped from $16 million in 1807 to just over $7 million in 1809 as a result of the embargo. Jefferson's political enemies complained that these losses were three times the cost of going to war. New England merchants were hardest hit, and protests erupted up and down the seaboard.

Jefferson even got hate mail on the subject. One letter from an unemployed Boston laborer read: "You Infernal Villain, How much longer are you going to keep this damned Embargo on to starve us poor people." The Federalists wittily observed that the embargo was like "cutting one's throat to cure the nosebleed."

To get around the embargo, southerners smuggled their goods out through Spanish Florida and New Englanders smuggled their goods into Canada. Jefferson responded by sending the army and navy to control the borders. They had to put down local rebellions wherever they went.

Jefferson hoped that the embargo would teach Americans to depend less on others and encourage them to invest in domestic production. To some extent it did, as capital and labor went into New England textiles and other manufacturing industries. Ultimately, however, the embargo was difficult and costly to enforce. Jefferson had to admit to his treasury secretary: "The embargo law is certainly the most embarrassing

one we have ever had to execute." It did postpone war, but only until the presidency of Jefferson's successor, James Madison.

In 1808, Jefferson was encouraged to run for a third term, but he turned it down, saying that he didn't want the presidency to become "an inheritance." He was 63 years old and looked forward to retirement. Considering the maelstrom of events in his public life, he had hardly had time to

James Madison, the fourth president of the United States, is sometimes called the "Father of the Constitution." He was its principal author.

grieve for his daughter Polly, who had died in 1804 from complications in childbirth. She had been just 25. He paid particular attention to her son, Francis Wayles Eppes, who was only three years old when she died.

On December 7, 1808, James Madison was elected president. A few days before he left office, Jefferson signed the Non-Intercourse Act, which effectively repealed the Embargo Act. It reopened trade with all nations except Britain and France. Like its predecessor, the Non-Intercourse Act did nothing to deter British and French aggression, and wrought havoc on the American economy. It was a factor leading up to the War of 1812.

Jefferson's popularity had sunk after the Embargo Act, but it was the general state of the world, including the viciousness of the press, that made the 65-year-old Jefferson long for retirement. He saw how complex the issues facing the nation were, and thought it best to leave it to the younger generation to resolve them.

> *"Nothing cn now be believed which is seen in a newspaper."*
>
> –Thomas Jefferson

During his presidency, Jefferson had exemplified his own democratic ideals. His casual manners were meant to show that he was not an aristocrat, but one of the people. He abandoned the European tradition of bowing, which was the way Washington and Adams had greeted people. Instead, Jefferson shook hands with his visitors, no matter who they were. Guests were shocked by this, and even more so by the tattered slippers Jefferson wore around the President's House. He called this approach pele-mele, which meant that no one got preferential treatment.

After he left office, Jefferson continued to live life as he had always known it at Monticello. He entertained many visitors, and his sister Martha Jefferson Carr moved in, along with her children. Patsy had seven children by then, so Jefferson, who once regretted having such a small family, was now surrounded by grandchildren.

PELE-MELE

Pele-mele is the French spelling of pell-mell, which describes something that is done in haste and confusion.

chapter **11**

The Illimitable Freedom of the Human Mind

R etirement was not a time for Jefferson to sit back in quiet reflection. He left office in massive debt, owing $30,000, and he had to make his plantations profitable. Work on a flour mill had begun, but it turned out to be a bad investment. Not long after its completion, a spring thaw flooded the dam that stored water for the mill.

The artist Rembrandt Peale painted this portrait of Jefferson. It is considered to be his masterpiece.

In 1812, Jefferson received a letter from John Adams that revived their friendship. Dr. Benjamin Rush, whose Bilious Pills had helped Lewis and Clark in times of trouble, had brought them together after a decade of estrangement by encouraging them to correspond. Adams was the first to break the silence.

Around this same time, Jefferson went to work creating the university of his dreams. For years, he had advocated public education in

Virginia at the elementary, secondary, and university levels, but each time he had proposed a bill, the General Assembly had voted it down.

In 1814, he was elected to the board of trustees of the Albemarle Academy. Jefferson envisioned a more important role for this small private school in Williamsburg. Working with Joseph Carrington Cabell, his man in the Virginia senate, Jefferson successfully petitioned to have Albemarle Academy transformed into a much larger institution called Central College. The "board of visitors" selected to manage the college included the current president of the United States, James Monroe, as well as his predecessors Jefferson and Madison.

The board of visitors approved Jefferson's architectural plan and began to raise money for the construction of the new campus. Jefferson was elected rector, or president, of the school, and he supervised construction of the "academical village" in Charlottesville.

Soon, Jefferson submitted a plan to the Virginia Assembly calling for a publicly supported primary school, secondary school, and university. Although this bill was shot down, Jefferson convinced the legislature that at the very least the state should have a full-fledged university, so that Virginia's best and brightest wouldn't flee north to institutions such as Harvard. He was given a mandate to establish the university, with a meager annual endowment of $15,000. In the summer of 1818, Jefferson, Madison,

The focal point of the University of Virginia campus, Jefferson's "academical village," was a rotunda that housed the library.

and Monroe met at Monticello to go over their plan for the university, which would be built on the site of Central College.

Charlottesville was an ideal central location for the university. And for Jefferson, its proximity to Monticello was also ideal—he observed its construction from a telescope at the house. Again, Jefferson was elected rector. For the next six years, he devoted himself to the construction of the University of Virginia and to the development of its curriculum. He also recruited its faculty.

Jefferson summed up his vision of the university as the "illimitable freedom of the human mind." This was reflected in the innovative design of the campus and its buildings, as well as its academic focus. Although most American universities were essentially seminaries—schools for the training of priests or ministers—Jefferson believed that education should be kept separate from religious instruction, and went so far as to ban the study of theology altogether.

At the school's inaugural banquet in 1824, Jefferson's old friend, the Marquis de Lafayette, toasted him as the "father" of the University of Virginia. Under Jefferson's guidance, the university rejected the traditional, classical curriculum for a broader one that included architecture, astronomy, philosophy, and political science. Jefferson, now 81, believed that educated citizens were essential to the survival of democracy.

Once the school opened, Jefferson enjoyed hosting Sunday dinners at Monticello for students and faculty. As long as Jefferson resided there, waves of guests practically ate him out of house and home. According to his overseer, Edmund Bacon, "They . . . came in gangs—the whole family, with carriage and riding-horses and servants; sometimes three and four such gangs at a time."

His daughter Patsy helped him entertain. She and her husband lived at Monticello, along with their 11 children. Poplar Forest, where Jefferson had found refuge in the overseer's house during the revolution, now provided a retreat from all the company. (He had started to build a house there during the second term of his presidency.)

Serpentine Walls

Serpentine (snake-like) walls line the 10 gardens in the University of Virginia. They were designed by Jefferson based on English "crinkle-crankle walls," which are more resistant to toppling than straight walls. In fact, a curved wall can be made of a single thickness of unreinforced brick, which makes it more economical than a straight wall as well.

The concerns of the young country followed Jefferson into retirement. As president, Jefferson had made many failed attempts to negotiate with Britain and France over their interference with American trade. By this time, America was fed up. Not only had Britain returned to its practice of impressment, it had also armed Indian tribes hostile to the United States.

Fighting started on the western front, where American Indians were sick of being pushed off their land. Two brothers from the Shawnee tribe—Tecumseh and Tenskwatawa—organized a multitribe resistance. When Tenskwatawa was killed, Tecumseh traveled to Canada and forged an open alliance with the British. The British were all too happy to stir up trouble for the Americans, who had declared war on June 18, 1812. Tecumseh struck a deal with General Isaac Brock, who placed him in command of all Indian forces.

The British won the Battle of Queenston Heights, fought in October 1812, but General Brock was killed in the conflict.

The Shawnee received a guarantee that if they won, the area known as the Old Northwest would become an independent Indian nation.

President Madison hoped to conquer all of Canada, which was still controlled by the British. He thought this would be easy, since the vast majority of British forces were tied up in European wars. In August, Jefferson wrote: "The acquisition of Canada this year, as far as the neighborhood of Quebec, will be a mere matter of marching, and will give us the experience for the attack on Halifax, the next and final expulsion of England from the American continent."

However, the British-Indian alliance soon proved otherwise. The alliance captured the Michigan and Illinois territories and placed them under British control. In the process, the Potawatomi Indians launched a bloody ambush called the Fort Dearborn Massacre, in which more than 50 Americans were killed. Then, in 1813, a 5,000-man U.S. army operation turned the tide, forcing the British to retreat.

Meanwhile, the Royal Navy had the American coastline blockaded. American farmers couldn't export their produce and were devastated. But small local factories were thriving, since they had to produce goods that used to be imported.

At around 8:00 PM on August 24, 1814, British troops marched into Washington, D.C. President Madison and his cabinet had fled to safety. The British soldiers remembered how American troops looted and burned the Canadian city of York the year before.

During the War of 1812, the British set fire to the White House, the Capitol building, and other buildings in Washington, D.C.

Dolley Madison had ordered the objects in the White House to be packed up and removed. Her foresight saved historically valuable silverware, books, clocks, curtains, and artwork. When the British arrived, they torched the White House, the Capitol, and several American warships. Unfortunately, the Library of Congress, which was housed in the Capitol, also went up in smoke, along with its 3,000 books.

Jefferson was at Monticello when he heard about the destruction. He had always had a close connection with the Library. He recommended books to buy, and had appointed the first two head librarians. Now, he offered to sell the government his own library, accumulated over 50 years, as a replacement, perhaps in part to help with his debts.

Congress approved the purchase in 1815 and paid $23,940 for 6,487 volumes. Jefferson ordered his overseer Edmund Bacon to pack the books into boxes, with the help of John Hemings and Burwell Colbert. They were transported to Washington on 16 wagons.

Unlike the original contents of the Library of Congress, which were mostly legal and economic in nature, Jefferson's library reflected his wide range of interests. It included books on architecture, art, science, literature, and geography, in English, French, Spanish, German, Latin, and Greek. Jefferson had even developed a system of arranging his books by subject, as opposed to alphabetically, as was commonly done. (In practice, he organized them by size.) In total, the collection contained twice the number of books that had been destroyed by the British.

Jefferson's books became the core of the present Library of Congress. But the man who wrote "I cannot live without books" almost immediately started buying more.

By this time, the War of 1812 was finally over. It had lasted three years, been fought on three fronts (Canadian, Atlantic, and southern), and claimed thousands of lives on both sides. The last battle was fought after Louisiana was invaded by 20,000 British soldiers, even though a peace treaty had already been signed. (The news traveled too slowly to prevent it.) The Americans, led by General Andrew Jackson, prevailed.

By 1819, the post-war United States fell into an economic depression, the effects of which reached Monticello. Jefferson could no longer sell land to pay his debts, because it was worth a quarter of its value a decade earlier, and there were no buyers. He even had to shut down his nail factory because he was unable to buy materials for it. Jefferson's reputation alone kept his creditors away.

chapter **12**

Spiritual Needs

Although it seems like Jefferson's jobs as trade minister, secretary of state, vice president, and president would have taken up all his energy, he never turned away from his intellectual pursuits. While he was secretary of state, he developed a wheel cipher, to code and decode messages. It came in handy in times of war because European postmasters had the habit of opening and reading all the letters that passed through their hands.

In the same week that he was inaugurated as vice president of the

Monticello had been Jefferson's home since 1770, but he made many changes over the years. A renovation begun in 1796 added terraces and a dome.

In Jefferson's study at Monticello is an invention known as a polygraph. When Jefferson wrote with one pen, the other made a copy. He kept copies of nearly all of the 20,000 letters he wrote in his lifetime.

United States, Jefferson was named president of the American Philosophical Society, a position he held for the next 18 years. That August, he presented a research paper on the megalonyx, a giant prehistoric sloth. In 1822, the extinct beast was named Megalonyx jeffersonii, after its discoverer.

Over the years, Jefferson kept busy with the design of many curiosities, including a revolving bookstand, a sundial, and the Great Clock that was installed at Monticello in 1804. Inspired by the Chinese gong, Jefferson intended the bell of the Great Clock to be heard all over the farm.

During the rare moments of quiet during his second term as president, Jefferson began writing a work on religion. In his retirement, he returned to it in earnest. As a child of the Enlightenment, Jefferson sought to erase the "ignorance and superstition" that enslaved people, even in their religious beliefs. He selected from the Bible "the very words only of Jesus," deleting parts of the gospels that he believed to be misinterpreted, and pulling from editions of the New Testament in different languages. The result was what he considered to be the essential moral teachings of Jesus. He finished *The Life and Morals of Jesus of Nazareth* in 1820. Though he didn't publish it, he shared it with friends.

Thomas Jefferson—his hair white and his hearing lost—sits hunched over his desk. Around him are plaster busts of the men he has admired and had the privilege to call friend: George Washington, Benjamin Franklin, and the Marquis de Lafayette. The man who has written thousands of pieces of correspondence is about to write his last one.

The country is a week away from celebrating the fiftieth anniversary of its independence. As one of the few surviving signers of the Declaration of Independence, Jefferson would be an honored guest at the party of Roger C. Weightman, mayor of Washington, D.C. He writes to decline the invitation because he isn't well enough to travel.

After months of illness, Jefferson has a feeling his time has come. His will has already been written out, leaving most of his property to his two grandsons, Francis Eppes and Thomas Jefferson Randolph. His "retirement library" is willed to the University of Virginia (though after his death, it will be sold to help pay off his debts). The will also frees his personal slaves—Burwell Colbert, the butler; John Hemings, a joiner; and Joseph Fossett, a blacksmith—bequeathing them a sum of money, as well as guaranteeing houses on his properties for them to live in. He might have freed all his slaves if his financial situation had allowed it. On the letter before him, he writes: "June 24, 1826." His writing hand is cramped with pain, never having recovered from the fracture it received in Paris. Or maybe it's just the rheumatism that has plagued his later years.

On the very anniversary of the country's independence, Jefferson died, at age 83. He had called his family in two days earlier for a farewell, and in the next two nights woke only to ask: "Is it the fourth?" He struggled to hang on until the Fourth of July. John Adams died the same day.

In his last days, Jefferson drew happiness from being surrounded by his family—especially his grandchildren, who adored him. His granddaughter Ellen Coolidge later described him as animated, cheerful, and affectionate. He often took the time to talk to them "as if we were much older and wiser people."

Finally, the lawyer, legislator, and statesman—who was so much more—ended his life recalling those thrilling days when the fate of a nation sat firmly in his hands. Although men like Patrick Henry stood up with stirring speeches, and others like George Washington fought the country's battles, there was an important place in history for this quiet, endlessly curious man.

The Jefferson Memorial in Washington, D.C., honors Jefferson and his famous words. In the background of this picture is an excerpt from the Declaration of Independence.

Events in the Life of Thomas Jefferson

December 16, 1773
Some 90,000 pounds
(41,000 kg) of tea
are thrown into the
harbor during the
Boston Tea Party.

June 1, 1779
Jefferson is elected
Governor of Virginia.

April 13, 1743
Thomas Jefferson
is born in
Goochland (later
Abermarle)
County, Virginia.

September 5, 1774
The First Continental
Congress convenes
in Philadelphia.

June 6, 1783
Jefferson is elected
to Congress.

June 28, 1776
Jefferson
submits his draft
Declaration of
Independence
to Congress.

September 6, 1782
Jefferson's wife,
Martha, dies
at age 33.

May 18, 1768
Jefferson begins to clear
land to build Monticello.

April 19, 1775
The Revolutionary War begins
with the Battles of Lexington
and Concord.

July 4, 1776
Congress accepts Declaration
of Independence.

May 7, 1784
Jefferson is appointed as
foreign minister in Paris.

March 4, 1801
Jefferson becomes
president at age 57.

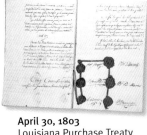

April 30, 1803
Louisiana Purchase Treaty
signed, adding 828,000
square miles (1,333,000
sq. km) of land to the
United States.

**August 31, 1803–
September. 23, 1806**
Lewis and Clark's
Corps of Discovery
expedition.

December 15, 1791
The Bill of Rights
is adopted.

July 14, 1789
Bastille Day;
start of the
French Revolution.

April 1, 1825
University of Virginia
officially opens.

July 2, 1788
The Constitution
of the United
States is ratified.

July 4, 1826
Jefferson dies
at Monticello
at age 83.

September 3, 1783
Treaty of Paris is
signed, officially
ending the
Revolutionary War.

Bibliography

Adams, Henry, and Harbert, Earl N., ed. History of the United States of America During the Administrations of Thomas Jefferson, 2 vols. New York: Literary Classics of the United States, 1986.

Adams, John and Adams, Abigail, Butterfield, L.H., Friedlaender, Marc, ed. The Book of Abigail and John: Selected Letters of the Adams Family, 1762-1764. University Press of New England: Lebanon, New Hampshire, 2002.

Bernstein, R. B. Thomas Jefferson. Oxford University Press: New York, 2003.

Betts, Edwin Morris, Ed. Thomas Jefferson's Farm Book. Chapel Hill: University of North Carolina Press, 1953.

"Economic Aspects of Tobacco During the Colonial Period 1612-1776." Tobacco.org. July 11, 2008.

Ferling, John. Adams vs. Jefferson: The Tumultuous Election of 1800. Oxford University Press: New York, 2005.

Hamilton, Alexander and Lodge, Henry Cabot, ed. The Works of Alexander Hamilton, 12 vols. G.P. Putnam & Sons: New York, 1886.

Hitchcock, Ripley. The Louisiana Purchase And the Exploration, Early History, and Building of the West. Boston: Ginn & Co., 1903.

Jefferson, Thomas. Summary View of the Rights of British America.

Jefferson, Thomas, Bergh, Albert Ellery, ed. The Writings of Thomas Jefferson. Vol. IX. Thomas Jefferson Memorial Association: Washington, D.C., 1907.

Jefferson, Thomas, and Ford, Paul Leicester, ed. The Works of Thomas Jefferson. New York and London: G.P. Putnam's Sons, 1905.

Jefferson, Thomas, and Shuffelton, Frank, ed. Notes on the State of Virginia. Penguin Books: New York, 1999.

Kaminski, John P., Jefferson, Thomas, and Cosway, Maria. Jefferson in Love: The Love Letters Between Thomas Jefferson and Maria Cosway. Lanham, MD: Rowman & Littlefield, 1999.

Lambeth, M.D., William Alexander and Manning, Warren Henry. Thomas Jefferson as an Architect and Designer of Landscapes. Houghton Mifflin Company: Boston and New York, 1912.

Lodge, Henry Cabot. American Statesmen: Alexander Hamilton. Houghton, Mifflin and Company: Boston, 1895.

"Martha Wayles Jefferson's account book." 2007. The Monticello Classroom. June 15, 2008.

McClellan, William Smith. Smuggling in the American Colonies. Department of Political Science of Williams College: New York, 1912.

"Monuments and Statues in Boston," by William Howe Downes. The New England Magazine, Nov. 1894, Vol. XI, No. 3.

Onuf, Peter S. Jeffersonian Legacies. University of Virginia Press, 1993.

Padover, Saul K. Jefferson. New York: New American Library, 1970.

Parton, James. Life of Thomas Jefferson, Third President of the United States. Boston: Houghton, Mifflin and Co., 1883.

Prucha, Francis Paul. The Great Father: The United States Government and the American Indians. Nebraska: University of Nebraska Press, 1986

Pierson, Rev. Hamilton W. and Bacon, Edmund. Jefferson at Monticello: The Private Life of Thomas Jefferson. New York: Charles Scribner, 1862.

Randall, Henry Stephens. The Life of Thomas Jefferson (3 vols). New York: Derby & Jackson, 1858.

Randolph, Thomas Jefferson, ed. Memoirs, Correspondence, and Private Papers of Thomas Jefferson. Vol. IV. Henry Colburn and Richard Bentley: London, 1829.

Randolph, Thomas Jefferson, ed. Memoirs, Correspondence and Miscellanies: from the Papers of Thomas Jefferson, vol. 1. F. Carr & Co.: Charlottesville, 1829.

Rayner, B.L. Life of Thomas Jefferson. Boston: Lilly, Wait, Colman & Holden, 1834.

Severance, John B. Thomas Jefferson: Architect of Destiny. New York: Clarion Books, 1998.

Smith, Margaret Bayard, and Hunt, Gallaird, ed. The First Forty Years of Washington Society. Charles Scribner & Sons: New York, 1906.

Stanton, Lucia C. Free Some Day: The African-American Families of Monticello. Chapel Hill: University of North Carolina Press, 2000.

Stephens, George M. Locke, Jefferson, and the Justices: Foundations and Failures of the U.S. Government. New York: Algora Publishing, 2002.

"Thomas Jefferson: First Inaugural Address." 1996. The Avalon Project at Yale Law School. June 24, 2008.

Voiland, Adam. "Clement Moore's Anonymous Screed Against Thomas Jefferson." US News and World Report. January 17, 2008.

"Washington D.C., 1800," EyeWitness to History, www.eyewitnesstohistory.com (2001).

Wildman, Mrs. Franklin B. "George Washington: The Commander In Chief." April 1966. Historic Valley Forge. Retrieved May 18, 2008.

Works Cited

"a people with whom in the early part of my life…" The Life of Thomas Jefferson, p. 12, vol. 1

"mouldy pies and excellent instruction" ibid. p. 18

"the favorite passion of my soul" The Life of Thomas Jefferson, p. 132, vol. 1.

"It is wonderful how much may be done if we are always doing." ibid. p. 474.

"No—if you have sowed your wild oats thus," ibid. p. 22.

"probably fixed the destinies of my life." Jefferson, p. 14

"polish of manner which distinguished him through life" The Life of Thomas Jefferson, p. 31, vol. 1.

"the elegant society which Governor Fauquier collected about him." ibid.

"Treason!" Thomas Jefferson: Architect of Destiny. p. 32; also Jefferson, p. 17.

"the only security against a burdensome taxation"

"ancient, legal, and constitutional rights" The Life of Thomas Jefferson, p. 79, vol. 1.

"No servants ever had a kinder master…" Jefferson at Monticello: The Private Life of Thomas Jefferson, p. 111.

"an attack on one colony…" Memoirs, Correspondence and Miscellanies, p. 6; also Jefferson, p. 26.

"kings are the servants, not the proprietors…" The Life of Thomas Jefferson, vol. 1, p. 97; also Jefferson, p. 27.

"Dispense, ye rebels!" Historic Valley Forge.

"This accident has cut off our last hopes of reconciliation." Memoirs, Correspondence and Miscellanies, p. 149; also Jefferson, p. 29.

"Don't fire until you see the whites of their eyes!" The New England Magazine, 1895, p. 367.

"For God's sake declare the colonies independent and save us from ruin." Locke, Jefferson, and the Justices, p. 53.

"The second day of July, 1776,…" The Book of Abigail and John, p. 142.

"Yes, we must, indeed, all hang together,…" Life of Thomas Jefferson, Third President of the United States, p. 192.

"the public would have more confidence in a military chief." The Life of Thomas Jefferson, vol. 1, p. 346.

"ten years of unchequered happiness." ibid., p. 385.

"The most easy ratio…" Memoirs, Correspondence, and Private Papers of Thomas Jefferson, p. 135.

"C'est vous qui replace M. Franklin?" The Works of Thomas Jefferson, p. 208.

"I never had seen so wretched an attempt at translation." The Life of Thomas Jefferson, vol. 1, p. 414.

"It was impossible for anything to be more ungracious." The Life of Thomas Jefferson, vol. 1, p. 445.

"…the most wretched style I ever saw." ibid., vol. 1, p. 447.

"We are now vibrating…" The Works of Thomas Jefferson, p. 385.

"would be a long story for the left (hand) to tell. " Jefferson in Love, p. 13.

"bewitched…by the British example" The Life of Thomas Jefferson, vol. 2, p.321.

"I am going to Virginia. I am then to be liberated…" Thomas Jefferson's Farm Book, p. xiii.

"the reign of witches" The Works of Thomas Jefferson, p. 432.

"…an experiment on the American mind…" The Life of Thomas Jefferson, vol. 2, p. 448.

"I have no ambition to govern men." ibid. p. 318.

"Jefferson is to be preferred." ibid., p. 583

"the most unfit man…" Adams vs. Jefferson, p. 180.

"The President's House is in a beautiful situation…" Eyewitness to History

"…a wise and frugal Government." The Writings of Thomas Jefferson, p. 320.

"the most insignificant office…" Thomas Jefferson, p. 117

"Unless something is done, and soon done, we shall be the murderers of our own children…the revolutionary storm, now sweeping the globe, will be upon us." The Writings of Thomas Jefferson, p. 418.

"…explore the Missouri River & such principal stream of it." The Works of Thomas Jefferson, p. 424

"…a thing beyond the constitution." ibid., p. 29

"Let us go on then perfecting it…" The Life of Thomas Jefferson, vol. 3, p. 71

"I renounce it with the greatest regret." The Louisiana Purchase, p. 73.

"Let the Land rejoice…" The Louisiana Purchase, p. 67.

"We shall, with great pleasure,…" The Life of Thomas Jefferson, vol. 3, p. 3.

"The embargo law is certainly the most embarrassing, …" The Works of Thomas Jefferson, p. 41

"academical village" The Works of Thomas Jefferson, p. 378

"They…came in gangs—the whole family,…" Jefferson at Monticello, p. 124.

"…illimitable freedom of the human mind,…" The Writings of Thomas Jefferson, p. 174.

"monkish ignorance and superstition,…" The Life of Thomas Jefferson, vol. 3, p. 541.

"…the very words only of Jesus,…" The Writings of Thomas Jefferson, p. 389.

Index

For Further Study

Jefferson's home, Monticello, is open to the public every day except Christmas. Photos, information, and original documents, such as letters written by slaves and Mrs. Jefferson's farm book, are available at Monticello Classroom at http://classroom.monticello.org

Monticello Explorer provides many resources, including a fascinating guided tour and 3D models of the house, available at http://explorer.monticello.org/index.html

The Library of Congress maintains the largest collection of original Jefferson documents in the world, including correspondence, financial account books, and drafts of documents. They're available at http://memory.loc.gov/ammem/collections/jefferson_papers/index.html

The Thomas Jefferson Digital Archive, maintained by the University of Virginia, contains 1,700 documents by or to Jefferson, including an interactive tour of his the university and a searchable collection of his views on various topics, available at http://etext.lib.virginia.edu/jefferson/

Acknowledgments

To my beloved Prentis, Scotia and Dagny, who allowed me to write; to Pholmarie Sewnaraine, who also allowed me to write; and to my wise and vigilant editors, Beth Hester and Beth Sutinis. A special thanks to Robin Gabriel, director of education at Monticello.

Picture Credits

FRONT COVER Photo by Getty Images

BACK COVER Photo by Alamy Images/North Wind Picture Archive

The photographs in this book are used with permission and through the courtesy of:

Corbis: pp. 1, 66T, 67, 110 Bettman; p. 64 The Corcoran Gallery of Art/Mrs. Benjamin Ogle Tayloe, p. 123TC. Bridgeman Art Library: pp. 3, 26, 38, 102 Massachusetts Historical Society; p. 19 Bridgeman Art Library; p. 27 Private Collection; p. 48 Brown University Library; p. 50 National Gallery, London; p. 56 Musee des Beaux Arts; pp. 81, 83 New-York Historical Society; p. 92 Musee Carnavalet; p. 94 Musee Franco Americaine; p. 95 Archives du Ministre des Affaires Etrangeres, p. 123TR. Thomas Jefferson Foundation: pp. 4-5, 35, 57, 61, 71, 122BL, TR. Architect of the Capitol: pp. 7, 55, 122BC, 123TL, 124-125, 126-127. Library of Congress: pp. 8, 11, 21, 33, 36, 39, 45, 66B, 76, 82, 84, 85, 86, 116, 122TL. The University of Virginia Art Museum: p. 9 Gift of Thomas Fortune Ryan. Colonial Williamsburg: pp. 14-15. SuperStock: pp. 16, 65, 87, 108; p. 24 Image Asset Management Ltd. ; p. 30 age footstock; p. 46 Huntington Library; p. 122TR. Virginia Historical Society: pp. 17, 20, 23, 42, 49, 123TR. Alamy Images: pp. 28, 69, 72, 96, 101 North Wind Picture Archive; p. 58 Mary Evans Picture Library; p. 113 Jason O. Watson; pp. 121, 123BR Dennis Hallinan. Getty Images: pp. 39, 44, 47, 51, 79, 90, 112, 119, 123TL, BC; p. 118 National Geographic. Art Resource: p. 59 Reunion des Musees Nationaux; p. 60 National Portrait Gallery, Smithsonian Institution; p. 100 American Art Museum. National Archives: pp. 62, 123BL. John Adams Historical Society: p. 74. DK Images: p. 80. American Antiquarian Society: p. 98. Library and Archives Canada: pp. 106, 114.

BORDER IMAGES from left to right:
Library of Congress, Getty Images, National Archives, Architect of the Capitol, North Wind Picture Archive, Library of Congress

About the Author

Jacqueline Ching wrote for *Newsweek* and the *Seattle Times* before editing books. She is the author of comic books and children's books, including *Abigail Adams: A Revolutionary Woman* and *The Assassination of Martin Luther King, Jr.*, for Rosen Publishing, and *Kim Possible* and *Pirates of the Caribbean* for Disney Publishing. Her husband is a comic-book artist for DC

Other DK Biographies you'll enjoy:

Marie Curie
Vicki Cobb
ISBN 978-0-7566-3831-3 paperback
ISBN 978-0-7566-3832-0 hardcover

Charles Darwin
David C. King
ISBN 978-0-7566-2554-2 paperback
ISBN 978-0-7566-2555-9 hardcover

Princess Diana
Joanne Mattern
ISBN 978-0-7566-1614-4 paperback
ISBN 978-0-7566-1613-7 hardcover

Amelia Earhart
Tanya Lee Stone
ISBN 978-0-7566-2552-8 paperback
ISBN 978-0-7566-2553-5 hardcover

Albert Einstein
Frieda Wishinsky
ISBN 978-0-7566-1247-4 paperback
ISBN 978-0-7566-1248-1 hardcover

Benjamin Franklin
Stephen Krensky
ISBN 978-0-7566-3528-2 paperback
ISBN 978-0-7566-3529-9 hardcover

Gandhi
Amy Pastan
ISBN 978-0-7566-2111-7 paperback
ISBN 978-0-7566-2112-4 hardcover

Harry Houdini
Vicki Cobb
ISBN 978-0-7566-1245-0 paperback
ISBN 978-0-7566-1246-7 hardcover

Helen Keller
Leslie Garrett
ISBN 978-0-7566-0339-7 paperback
ISBN 978-0-7566-0488-2 hardcover

Joan of Arc
Kathleen Kudlinksi
ISBN 978-0-7566-3526-8 paperback
ISBN 978-0-7566-3527-5 hardcover

John F. Kennedy
Howard S. Kaplan
ISBN 978-0-7566-0340-3 paperback
ISBN 978-0-7566-0489-9 hardcover

Martin Luther King, Jr.
Amy Pastan
ISBN 978-0-7566-0342-7 paperback
ISBN 978-0-7566-0491-2 hardcover

Abraham Lincoln
Tanya Lee Stone
ISBN 978-0-7566-0834-7 paperback
ISBN 978-0-7566-0833-0 hardcover

Nelson Mandela
Lenny Hort & Laaren Brown
ISBN 978-0-7566-2109-4 paperback
ISBN 978-0-7566-2110-0 hardcover

Mother Teresa
Maya Gold
ISBN 978-0-7566-3880-1 paperback
ISBN 978-0-7566-3881-8 hardcover

Annie Oakley
Chuck Wills
ISBN 978-0-7566-2997-7 paperback
ISBN 978-0-7566-2986-1 hardcover

Pelé
Jim Buckley
ISBN 978-0-7566-2987-8 paperback
ISBN 978-0-7566-2996-0 hardcover

Eleanor Roosevelt
Kem Knapp Sawyer
ISBN 978-0-7566-1496-6 paperback
ISBN 978-0-7566-1495-9 hardcover

George Washington
Lenny Hort
ISBN 978-0-7566-0835-4 paperback
ISBN 978-0-7566-0832-3 hardcover

Laura Ingalls Wilder
Tanya Lee Stone
ISBN 978-0-7566-4508-3 paperback
ISBN 978-0-7566-4507-6 hardcover

Look what the critics are saying about DK Biography!

"…highly readable, worthwhile overviews for young people…" —*Booklist*

"This new series from the inimitable DK Publishing brings together the usual brilliant photography with a historian's approach to biography subjects." —*Ingram Library Services*